Insight In Sight

Was I Born Like This?

Sylvie Haché

Insight In Sight
Was I Born Like This?
by Sylvie Haché

Printed in the United States of America

ISBN 9781613790977

www.xulonpress.com

Dedication

I dedicate this book to everyone who has ever said, "I was born gay", "God made me this way", or "It's just the way I am"; and to all the parents, friends and family who have heard this proclamation from a loved one.

I also dedicate this book to those who question their own sexual preference or orientation, (as well as to the parents, legal guardians, friends, and family who care about them).

In addition, I dedicate this book to government officials that support non-straight rights as well as those that wonder whether they should or not.

Finally, I dedicate this book to school principals, teachers, counselors, social workers and anyone else with the authority and power to guide young minds to make the right decision as they struggle with this type of question.

When we have a willingness to open up our minds to new knowledge, insight and possibilities, we can discover a whole new world that is even better than we could have hoped for or imagined.

Acknowledgement

I would like to thank my parents, Leo and Yvette for your wisdom, insight, support and unconditional love. It has been instrumental in shaping who I have become. You have both represented fairness, forgiveness and how important it is to help others. I love, honor and respect you both.

I am grateful to both of my children, Logan and Monika. You have truly been, and continue to be a blessing. You bring great joy and happiness into my life, and fill my heart with love.

Lastly, and most importantly, I thank God for giving me my life back—literally!

Table of Contents

Introduction

T he fight for non-straight rights has remained the same for years—to have the freedom to love another without discrimination. To support this cause, many have suffered humiliation, judgment, ridicule, pain, and even death. In an attempt to rectify this, society has been persuaded, and laws have been amended, to accept and protect the non-straight lifestyle.

While actively living a non-straight lifestyle, I would keep my guard up to anything that might sound as though it could potentially come against me. I believed people were either for me or against me—there was no middle ground. However, after years of living this way, I was unexpectedly met with challenges and losses I could not guard myself against—nor could the law protect me.

Now that I have experienced all this, I have gained insight that I had not been aware of prior to experiencing it. I have learned we can opt to do absolutely anything we want to do—

that is our free will choice; likewise, we can live our lives any way we choose. Still, we need to be aware that although all things are permissible for us, not all things are profitable.

This story is about my journey leading from being straight (the way I began), into living my life as a homosexual, to what caused me to take inventory of my life and place me in a position to share what I have learned, with you.

We can fight for any freedom. I have learned, if we can get enough back-up, interest, and people to support our cause, we can be granted legal rights and privileges to change any current legislation. However, just because we receive the right to do something, does not mean we are nullified from the natural consequences. We currently have the legal privilege to smoke cigarettes and drink alcohol once we reach a certain age, but that does not protect us against the potential harmful effects of practicing such rights. Sometimes the natural consequences of our privileges are evidently clear (such as the case with cigarette smoking, as it relates to lung cancer), and other times they are not. Even after it has been proven that cigarette smoking is linked with cancer, there are still those who choose to smoke, some of which end up with lung cancer. As a result, many of them suffer humiliation, judgment, ridicule, pain, and even death—all because they choose to exercise their legal right to smoke.

Point being, I have come to understand there are correct choices we can make that will bring us good results; equally, there are incorrect choices that will bring us grief and undesirable results. I have learned that our own personal opinion about what is right and wrong is truly insignificant. Any one of us can have an opinion that it is a good choice to smoke cigarettes, and feel justified because the law grants us that privilege, but that still will not change the truth about whether or not it is the correct thing to do. Likewise, just because there are those who support a certain right or option for us to embrace, that does not shield us against the resulting natural consequences of exercising such a right.

I am compelled to share my journey and this information with you because a great deal of the unexpected challenges and losses I faced resulted out of the rights I fought for, was granted, and chose to exercise.

I once heard it said, "The power of truth is that we must either submit to it or rebel against it. There is no neutral ground." So what exactly is the truth? What exactly is the power behind the truth? And where do we find the real, untainted truth? If we have the choice to either submit to it or rebel against it, then truth in and of itself must be in existence. If truth has power, it would be wise for us to find out what affect it can have on our life.

I encourage you to open your eyes, mind, and heart to the information I share. I offer it to bring you to the place where you truly enjoy your life, in full abundance.

It is still our choice to live our life as we desire. Therefore, I am not suggesting which option you should choose for yourself; that is up to you. However, the information contained within should offer you hope to reach that decision with clarity and understanding.

This book is not about judgment. It is about awareness, options, and information provided for your own personal safety and protection. It is only through making correct choices that we can receive protection against the natural consequences, and be guarded against unnecessary pain and loss.

If you are considering whether a non-straight lifestyle is right for you, the information contained within will provide you with knowledge to help you reach that final decision. If you are currently living a non-straight way of life (regardless of which category you might consider yourself in), it is my desire to share this knowledge with you that I believe is vitally important for you to be aware of. The outcome of not knowing this, can impact depths of your life you may not even be aware could be affected.

It is my hope that once you receive the insight in sight, you will know for sure whether or not you were born like this. Then you can rest assured, knowing you are making the best lifestyle choice for yourself, your family, and your future.

Chapter One

Ready For a Change

New mission in life.

It was 1:30 a.m. when my father picked up the phone and asked, with panicked voice, "What am I supposed to do?"

My mother, on the other end of the line, simply said, "Just let her go." I saw uncertainty and doubt rise up in my father's eyes. As he hung up the phone, he looked at me and, for the first time, appeared dumbfounded. He rummaged in his pants pocket and pulled out a twenty-dollar bill.

"Here, take this," he said as he handed it to me. "That's all I have to give to you." At that moment, I saw a look of fear come over his face. He was clearly torn. Should he stop me or let me go? The tears that welled up in his eyes led me to believe he wondered if he would ever see me again.

I paused for a moment and gave him a big hug. "Thanks Dad, I love you," I said as I kissed him on the cheek. Then I grabbed my suitcases and quickly made my way out the front door to the taxi waiting for me outside.

I was returning to the venue from where I had just come, where Colleen and the others waited for me to return. I hoped I would not be too late. As the taxi pulled up, I saw the buses out back and sighed in relief. As I gathered my belongings, I noticed Colleen talking to one of the band members. She waved at me. I smiled back at her. I paid the taxi driver with the money my father had given me and the taxi drove off.

Although I had never done anything like this before, I was ready for whatever this adventure might bring. I went over to Colleen. We stood silently next to each other; we had nothing really to say. I looked around as I watched the crew busily pack up all the sound and lighting equipment, loading it up into the huge transport trucks. I felt like I was in the middle of a movie. In fact, this entire evening had felt that way. When I had arrived at the concert hours earlier, I knew no one. In fact, I did not know anyone in this small town. I had arrived at my father's doorstep earlier that same day.

As I stood there, the cool crisp September air chilled me. I gathered my unzipped jacket a bit more tightly around my waist. I had always liked September because I really enjoyed going to school, but this year there was no reason for me to return. Two months prior, I had graduated high school and completed one year of business administration.

That is when I made the decision to leave the small town I had grown up in to head out to the big city. This was my new mission in life. Where exactly would I go? I was not sure. I just knew I needed and was ready for a change. That is what led me to this moment.

There's a band playing tonight.

Earlier that morning, a few guy friends I knew were driving out of my hometown in Nova Scotia, headed towards a place in New Brunswick. They agreed to take me along and drop me off at my father's house on the way.

I had not seen my father much since my parents separated five years prior. I had spent a great deal of time commuting with him when I was 14 years old, when I had the urge to start working out. We would drive onto the Air Force base every night. He would work in the hobby shop, building things. I would spend the same amount of time at the recreation center, lifting weights. I was the only girl in the gym at the time, so I just followed the guys' routine and sat down at the equipment after their set. I could not be bothered to adjust the weights, so I ended up bench pressing 120 pounds and leg-pressing the entire stack of 500 pounds for five sets of ten. I became very strong *(for a girl)*, and loved the feeling of power and strength—it made me feel safe and invincible.

When we arrived at the entrance gate barricading admittance onto the Air Force base, I knew to call my dad and he would come get me since I had never been there before and did not know my way around. A few minutes later, my dad showed up. I transferred into his car and we drove to his barracks. Our conversation was somewhat strained, but I promised him I would just be passing through until I could figure out what I was planning to do next.

The truth was, I had no plan whatsoever and no idea of what I even wanted to do. I just had a goal to move to the big city, and somehow I had decided to leave all the other details up to chance.

"Here we are," my father announced as we arrived at his barracks. It was extremely small, barely suitable for one person, practically impossible for two for any length of time. I was thankful my father was gracious enough to overlook the cramped quarters and allowed me to stay with him until I could figure out my next move, but I also felt a sense of urgency to make a decision soon.

"I heard there's a band playing tonight on base and I thought you might be interested in going," he said.

"Who's playing?"

He did not know, but let me know that if I was interested, he could arrange for some young Privates on base to take me there and bring me back when it was over. I was fine with that.

I was not sure how to spend the next three hours waiting for the concert to start, so I decided to unpack my bags. I took my time unpacking. I could feel my father's eyes upon me as I tried to find suitable places to hang all my things. Once finished unpacking, I got myself ready for the concert.

There was a knock at the door. I opened it to find three young service men dressed in casual attire. "Are you ready?" they asked.

"Yes," I replied, as I wished my father a good night.

Do you have a backstage pass?

The guys introduced themselves as we all piled into the car and drove ten minutes to the other side of the base. As soon as we pulled up, I could hear the music playing. I did not recognize the group but was pumped because I liked the sound. I strode ahead of the guys and headed towards the entrance. Opening the door, I could see it was packed. No one was sitting. It was a gym converted into a makeshift concert venue for the night. "Do you want a drink?" one of the guys asked, pointing towards the provisional bar in the corner.

"No, I'm good," I answered, barely looking at him. I did not drink alcohol, so as he headed towards the bar with his buddies, I proceeded to make my way through the crowd. Although I had been to several concerts before, I always had a seat in the stands and never had the opportunity to see a band up close and personal. Since this venue was different from all the rest, I decided to venture up and make my way closer to the front. By now, the guys that brought me were nowhere in sight. I did not really care to find them.

I had just broken up with my boyfriend of three years, Patrick, because I felt I needed to venture out into this great big world to figure out what life was all about and, hopefully, to find myself in the process. Not having any of the guys in my space, expecting me to somehow conform to their group mentality, was exactly what I needed right now.

As I got closer to the front of the stage, my eyes fell on the drummer. I cannot explain it, but he had my complete and undivided attention. He was blonde, attractive, and as I stood there staring at him, he appeared to be smiling and staring directly back at me. After each song they played, I inched my way closer to the front of the stage. At one point, while I was staring right at him, he turned his head to the side of the stage and yelled out something to someone off stage that only that person could hear. Then he looked back at me, as though to point me out, then quickly back to the person standing on the side of the stage. I saw a man's face peer out from the edge of the stage. He and the drummer were having an entire conversation as the band played on. Finally, their chat over, the drummer resumed his focus on the drums and on leading the audience in cheers and shouts as he lay into a drum solo.

I had never heard any of their songs before, but I was drawn in, intrigued by the entire atmosphere. I wished that somehow, this moment would never end. Just then, I got a tap on my shoulder. I stopped staring at the drummer long enough to turn my attention to the large security guard who had tapped me. He was dressed in black, had a headset linked to one ear, and carried a clipboard in one hand, a walkie-talkie in the other. "Do you have a stage pass?" he yelled.

"A what?" I yelled back.

"A backstage pass!"

I shook my head no, thinking I might have somehow gotten too close to the front of the stage. I took a step back to get behind whatever boundary he might be enforcing.

"Do you want one?" he asked, while pointing behind him towards the side of the stage.

I was stunned. "Okay," was all I could say.

He smiled at me and motioned for me to follow him.

He opened the door at the side of the stage and led me up a small flight of stairs. "Here, put this on," he said as he handed me a large square fabric pass that stated the tour band names, along with that night's date printed on it. I peeled off the backing and stuck it to my top.

"I'm Colleen," shouted a girl who had been standing backstage. "I'm touring with the band," she proclaimed. I was surprised, intrigued, and then...jealous. *That sounded like so much fun! I wish I could travel with the band!* "Why don't you ask if you can come along?" she asked. The awestruck look on my face no doubt prompted her to continue. "Just ask Steve, the Backstage Manager at the end of this set," she instructed me. I nodded, not really knowing what else to do.

Suddenly, she pointed over my shoulder, causing me to turn around and look. I gasped. There I was on one side of the actual stage! I inconspicuously peered out over the side and watched as the crowd raised their hands up in the air, smiling, shouting and singing along. I felt a wave and rush permeating from that audience that seemed to envelop the performers. The louder the crowd cheered, the more energy the band put out. I stood there fascinated, enthralled, and caught up in the whole atmosphere. Soon their set was over and the band members exited the stage.

"Go ask him; he's over there," Colleen prompted as she pointed to Steve. I made my way over.

"I was wondering if I could tour with the band?"

"Let me get back to you," he said. I nodded. Then he spoke on his walkie-talkie and proceeded to do what he needed to do.

I went back over and stood by Colleen. "What'd he say?" she asked. I told her I had to wait to find out.

"Have you been touring with the band for long?" I asked. She shook her head no and said she had joined them at their last concert date.

I cannot find them.

Just then, the crowd roared with anticipation as the members of the second band swiftly passed by me and found their place on stage. The audience went wild with excitement. I had never heard of this band before but could tell the audience was familiar with them. The crowd bellowed out the name of the group in unison. I lost all sense of awareness as I became captivated in the thrill of it all. With camera in hand I focused and pointed to this all-female band. Unexpectedly one of the band members came over towards me and posed for a photo as she strummed her electric guitar—as only a rock star would do. The flashes from my camera bathed her in stardom light. The lead singer introduced the members of the band. She finished with herself stating a very unusual yet evident Hollywood name.

As I stood dazed and amazed, I got another tap on the shoulder—it was Steve. He told me I could travel with them but I would need to be ready to go in one hour. I snapped back to, with a chill of excitement.

"He said yes!" I yelled at Colleen.

"Go get your stuff!" she said, as if reminding me of what I needed to do.

I knew I needed to get a taxi back to my dad's place, only I did not remember exactly where he lived or how to get back there. I had not bothered to write down his address and I had left his phone number back in the room. I would have to find one of the guys to take me back there but I could barely remember what any of them looked like. The hair on all the guys on base was buzzed off, so they all looked pretty much the same. I hoped that by walking through the crowd, one of them would recognize me.

I waded through the crowd trying to find them. Unsuccessful, I walked outside thinking they might have stepped out for a smoke. Nope! They were not out there, at least I did not see them and none of them spotted or came over to me. I went back inside and made my way to the front of the hall, hoping that one of them would see me, but to no avail. Almost half an hour passed.

I made my way back to the stage door and, with my back-stage pass clearly visible, entered without a problem. "I can't find them!" I shouted in a panic to Colleen.

"Come on, I'll help you!" she yelled back.

Together, we worked our way back through the crowd. I was unsure what she could do to help, but then she grabbed hold of my arm, which seemed to catch people's attention. When she reached down to hold my hand, even more people noticed us. The crowd seemed to spread out of our way as more people stared and pointed at us.

"There you are!" came a voice from behind me. It was one of the guys.

"I need to get back to my dad's immediately," I shouted.

Colleen released her grip on my hand. Uncertain why I was asking to go home, he simply signaled for a taxi and directed him where to take me. When I arrived back at the barracks, I asked the taxi to wait for me, and then ran down the long corridor that led to my father's room. I knocked on the door frantically.

"Hi dad," I tried to whisper, both because of the hour and because it was obvious I had just woken him up. "I gotta' go!" I said as I raced against time. With both hands, I grabbed everything I had meticulously unpacked and tossed them back into my bag haphazardly.

As I tried to close the zipper, my father struggled to gather information. "What do you mean you gotta' go?" he asked.

"I'm travelling with the band," I told him, letting him know the only way I could do that was to ensure I would get back in time. I glanced at the clock across the room, which let me know I now had only ten minutes to get back.

I had said little, but enough to render my dad speechless. "Wait a minute," he instructed me (as only a father can). That is when he picked up the phone to call my mother and she told him to let me go.

As I headed down the corridor my bags in tow, my dad summoned one final request, "Promise you'll call me or your mom to let us know you got there safely."

"Okay Dad, I promise," I yelled back over my shoulder in a loud whisper. I ran on to start my new life.

We were in for an unexpected surprise.

When I returned, I saw Colleen smiling and waving at me.

"It's time," Steve announced.

I grabbed my stuff and boarded the bus. The front of the bus had benches on each side, facing one another. Each could seat eight people comfortably. Beyond that, that were rows of bunks three high and two across, allowing room for twelve to sleep. In the very back was a soundproof booth with a bench all the way around it, and a table that could collapse and fold down in the middle. This would be a temporary home for Colleen and me.

We were officially groupies. Each day they gave us new badges as subtle reminders of our status. The badges granted us free access, free meals, and the occasional hotel room at night to share with female members of the crew. Each morning, the bus would arrive at a new location and the crew would get busy working hard and setting up for that night's performance. Colleen and I spent our days touring the towns of each new location, going into shops and stores, and just looking around. Then we would go back to the bus, sit in the soundproof booth in the back and crank up the stereo.

At night, we would go to the concert where the bands played to sold out crowds. We savored the freedom to go anywhere we desired within the stadiums. The passes we pretentiously wore, granted us that privilege. Colleen would often mingle with people in the crowd, as she stood on one side of the barrier, and they were restricted to standing on the other side. She liked the feeling of that power. I preferred to stand up on the edge of the stage, like I had done that first night. I loved the liveliness and excitement of the crowd; their energy permeated within me and gave me a natural high.

On the fourth night, we arrived at a huge hotel in Montreal. Shortly after we reached our room, Steve knocked on our door. "Hey ladies, follow me," he said. Intrigued, we both followed his lead. He brought us to another room and opened the door to a foyer, which led to four other doors. "Wait here," he instructed. He entered one of the four doors. I had no clue what was about to happen. We were left waiting for a good half hour.

Then he opened the door and a woman walked out with her hair disheveled, and her clothes a mess.

"You're next," he said as he pointed to me, motioning for me to enter.

I got up and walked toward the door Steve held open. I looked inside to see the drummer lying on a king-sized bed, motioning for me to lie down beside him. My heart skipped a beat, but not in a good way. Although I was attracted to him, I was not at all comfortable with what he was obviously pro-posing. Suddenly, I was aware of what he and all the rest of them were expecting in return for allowing me to travel on the road with them.

"I can't do this," I told Steve, as I quickly wiggled out of his grip and ran back to our room. Colleen quickly followed.

"We gotta' go," I said. I was not willing or prepared to make that lifestyle choice, to pay my way through life like that. I knew then that our time on the tour would soon end.

We would be in Toronto the following day. Colleen let me know she had an aunt there and that she would arrange for us to stay with her for a few days.

The following morning, we got back on the bus, but now we had to pay for our food. When we finally arrived in Toronto, Colleen and I both grabbed our bags and got off the bus. Steve approached us, "Hey, no hard feelings, we just thought you ladies knew what was expected." Surprisingly, he invited us to join the band and crew at a posh bar in Yorkville for a private pre-concert party before that night's performance. Colleen's aunt would not be home until later that evening, so having nowhere else to go, we both accepted.

When we arrived at the bar, we entered in through the restaurant on the main floor. It was packed. There were white linen tablecloths on the tables and blue-gray paint on the walls. Crystal light fixtures hung off the ceiling. The light streaming in from the two walls that faced the street gave it an elegant feel. Steve led us through to a set of stairs. We walked up to the next level. There we found a dance club. The band had reserved this space for their private party. I thought this was our final destination, but Steve led us towards the back and up yet another staircase into the attic. There we were met by an unexpected surprise. "What's this?" I questioned Steve.

"Any kind of drug you want." He replied, as he held my arm and led me closer to the tables. There were two large tables with white tablecloths on them topped with all types of drugs. Cocaine lay prepped in rows on a mirrored tile. "Help yourselves ladies," Steve said with a smile.

I was shocked and not at all interested so I just nodded, thanked him, and began to back out. Colleen, on the other hand, approached the tables with curiosity, obviously tempted. I nudged her, urging her to leave the room with me but she refused. She wanted to try some. "Come on Colleen, we have to leave now!" I pressed as I tried to pull her out of the room. Steve still had a hold of my arm. So as I had already done once before, I wiggled my way out from Steve's grip; then I quickly escorted Colleen down the stairs, out the front door and into the street. I knew it was getting late and we needed to get to her aunt's place before dark.

You need a place to live?

We reached her aunt's place and she welcomed us in. She graciously invited us to stay for a couple of days. The next few days, Colleen and I set about figuring out our game plan. We ventured down Yonge Street, the main strip, when Colleen stopped in front of an exotic dance club. "I've never been inside one of these before," she said. I had never been in such a place either. The sign out front advertised guys danced downstairs and ladies danced on the main floor. Uncertain what to expect but curious, we both stepped inside.

We were met by a bouncer. "You ladies want to go downstairs?" he asked. Nodding our heads, he pointed us to the back of the club. We both responded uncomfortably as we passed the female dancers. We both tried looking away, holding our heads low as we scurried to the back of the club and made our way down the stairs. To our surprise, it was empty. I was relieved.

There were booths on either side of what appeared to be a dance floor in the center. Colleen and I both sunk down into a booth. It had been a long five days and we were both exhausted. With no jobs, no money, no future plans and soon, no home, we both wondered what we were going to do. We tossed around some ideas.

Just then, a woman popped her head up over the adjoining booth. "Did I hear you ladies say you needed a place to live?" We both nodded in unison. "I've got just the place. I live in a flat where two rooms just became available." If we needed jobs she said we could work there as dancers. I was not at all interested in becoming a dancer, so flatly refused. Colleen, however, considered the woman's offer. As the two of them began talking about what it was like to be a dancer, my mind began to wonder what was truly important to me.

Although it was evidently clear temptation to get whatever I wanted or needed by illegal, unethical, or immoral means could be found lurking around almost every corner; I vowed to myself that I would not venture down that path. I was bound and determined to make choices I was certain would not mess up my life.

The next day, we went to look at the flat and moved in the same day. I called my dad to let him know I had arrived safely. When I asked Colleen if she had contacted her parents to notify them of her safe arrival, she let me know she had not, nor was she interested in doing so.

A few days later, I got a job waitressing. Colleen became an exotic dancer. A month later, she let us know she had a new boyfriend and was moving in with him. I moved out about two months after that when my ex-boyfriend Patrick surprised me by showing up unannounced on my front doorstep. We decided to move in to our own place since the one room in the flat was clearly too small for both of us.

Patrick was a real nice guy, which was the problem. I wanted adventure in my life. I wanted to be daring and launch out into the unknown. I just believed if I stayed with him, that somehow I would miss out. A few months later, we broke up.

I ran into the woman Chrystal and I had shared a flat with at the local grocery store a few months later. I found out Colleen was then six months pregnant, a cocaine addict, and that her boyfriend had kicked her out on the street. I never saw Colleen again.

I thought back to that day when I left my father standing there as I ran off to start my new life. I recalled how he had pleaded for me to call him to assure him I was safe. I had not comprehended the depth of his concern until I learned how Colleen's life was ending up. Her parents had no idea what happened to their daughter, I was sure. I was grateful I had avoided making the same poor lifestyle choices she had.

Chapter Two

Old Beginning

As long as you promise not to kill anyone.

A few months later on a cold November night, I was working as a server at a classy Fisherman's Warf Restaurant and bar down by the waterfront. It was a popular summer hangout and boasted the joys of summer with its fishing and boating décor and paraphernalia. One room was filled with circular wooden tables adorned with seashells and starfish imbedded into the thick veneer coating. Large wooden captain's chairs surrounded each table. Wooden paddles were among the nautical and fishing images on the walls. An old wooden fishing boat hung from the ceiling and a huge iron anchor arched majestically above the entranceway. Tea light candles in little yellow holders adorned each table, giving the whole room a peaceful mellow summer's nightglow.

It was a quiet night with only two tables to serve, so I occupied myself by becoming more familiar with the servers ordering computer. As my back was turned and I was deep in thought, a man spoke from behind me, "May I have a knife?"

Without even turning around, I answered back smiling, "As long as you promise not to kill anyone." I grabbed a butter knife from below the service station and turned to hand it to him. As our eyes met, I lost my breath. He was the most gorgeous man I had ever laid eyes on. He was tall, blonde, had a muscular physique, and the most captivating blue eyes. I felt a slight tug as he tried to take the knife out of my hand. Embarrassed, I released my grip. He thanked me and walked back to the bar where he had been sitting.

From the corner of my eye, I watched as he finished his meal, and then lay the cloth napkin beside his plate. His back was towards me, so he could not see me looking at him. Then he started to get up. I turned my head away quickly to avoid being caught staring at him. I so wished he would not leave. In short, I felt very attracted to him. He caught me off guard when he said, "I was wondering if you'd like to go out for coffee?"

"I don't drink coffee." True enough.

"Alright," he said as he turned around and walked back to the bar. A few moments later, he came back over to me. "Would you like to go out for tea?"

"I don't drink tea either." This was true also. When he turned away, now for the second time, I realized it was not about the coffee or the tea and offered, "I do drink juice."

A smile came over his face. "Okay then, juice it is." He sat back down at the bar to finish his drink.

Strike three, you're out!

The restaurant was close to empty and I had given the bill to my single remaining table. I made my way over to where he was sitting to introduce myself and to ask a few questions. His name was Jake. "Where'd you get the tan?" I asked, curious. Since summer was already more than a wish away. He explained that he had just returned from Florida. He had driven an elderly woman there and then decided to stay there a few days. "Is that what you do for a living?" I asked. He shook his head. He was a firefighter.

Just then, I heard another man's voice behind me: "You will have his son—blonde hair, blue eyes." I whipped my head around to see who would say something like that. Nobody was there.

"Are you alright?" he asked.

I assured him I was fine and let him know I thought I had heard something behind me. I did not dare tell him what I had heard—he would think I was nuts! Maybe I was I thought; nothing like that had ever happened to me before.

It was nearing closing time, so he offered to take me for that juice after my shift. I agreed this time was as good as any, cashed out quickly, and then met him standing just outside the front door. We got into his car and drove to a 24-hour coffee shop.

We spent this time getting to know one another a bit better. He was funny, yet intelligent and I really enjoyed his company. There came a point when he let me know there was something he needed to tell me. I had no idea what he would say, so I braced myself. He told me he had been married once. I thought, *strike one*. Then he told me that he had a 3-year old daughter from that marriage. I thought, *strike two*. He pulled a pack of cigarettes out of his jacket pocket and lit one. I thought, *strike three, you are out*. He took a drag, excused himself and went to the washroom.

As I watched him walk away, I questioned myself. Why would I be ready to drop him so quickly? After all, he had a stable job, he had been married once before (so he was clearly the marrying kind), and he had a child (something I looked forward to in the future). Since I did not know much about parenting, he could surely offer some help. With these new thoughts, I cancelled out all the strikes and decided to see where this might lead.

I knew it would work.

We spent a lot of time together and grew close very quickly. We worked out together and talked about future plans and goals. Since he was five years older than me, he had experienced things I had not, such as dealing with money and buying property. He would make suggestions and recommendations for our future aspirations and I would simply agree with him, therefore, we never quarreled.

By December, we decided to go on a ski trip to Vermont. He had vacation time from work and the restaurant had reduced my shifts to one a week, so we were both free to go.

When we got to the ski hill, he handed someone a camera to take a picture of us. Then he stood behind me and wrapped his arms around me. I smiled sheepishly as I realized this was the closest we had been.

He was an expert skier but I was a novice, so soon after we arrived, I managed to fall over the front of my skies and twisted my ankle severely. Sadly, this cut our ski vacation short. On the return home, we decided to take a detour to visit my mom.

We arrived at my mother's place and he went up to the front door and rang the doorbell. My mother opened the door and was shocked to find me cradled in his arms as he stood there, lifting me, as though we were a married couple crossing the threshold. He was obviously quite strong and that made me feel very safe with him. "I twisted my left ankle skiing," I told her.

She directed Jake to place me on the sofa in the living room as she proceeded to give me some health supplements. She grasped my left hand and proceeded to perform reflexology on it. Jake was dumbfounded and clearly did not know what to think. He had never heard of this practice before but I had grown up with it, so I knew it would work—and it did. The following morning, I was able to walk without pain. "I didn't know you were a health nut," he said.

"I'm not," I responded, "I just live a healthy lifestyle."

A few days later, we left and returned home.

Let's go out and celebrate.

It seemed to me Jake and I had a perfect relationship—except for the fact that he smoked. I longed to live my life with him and hoped he felt the same way about me.

On Wednesday nights, after our workout, we went out for chicken wings at our favorite pub. On this particular night, all the tables were full, so we agreed to sit at the bar. The bartender got Jake a beer and I got my usual club soda with lime. Jake seemed deep in thought and began to tell me how much he cared about me. He asked if I would consider marrying him. I was speechless—I wanted to, but was hesitant. "What seems to be the problem?" he asked.

"I just can't marry someone who smokes."

He immediately turned and looked away from me. He dropped his head to his chest, and then fondled the package of cigarettes that lay before him. Taking a deep haul from his lit cigarette, he stared blankly into his own reflection in the mirror on the back wall, through the multitude of assorted alcohol bottles that lined it. A few minutes later, he pulled out two cigarettes from his almost full pack and meticulously laid them side by side before closing the package. The bartender's eyes met mine. I could tell he was as curious as I was to see what was about to transpire, since we were the only two sitting at the bar and it was clear he had overheard our conversation.

Jake proceeded to light the first cigarette with the butt of the one he was ready to put out. He did not say a word, nor did I. I felt no need to. The three of us just sat there waiting for the cigarette to expire into a cloud of smoke. With each drag, the smoke encircled Jake's head.

Jake lit his last cigarette. Continuing in silence, I preoccupied myself by drinking my club soda, now warm. He hauled on that cigarette as though it would be his last one. Then, with a final exhale, he blew the last of the white smoke towards his reflection in the mirror and butted it out. He picked up his already closed cigarette pack and, in one swift purposeful flick, propelled it like a Frisbee, landing it dead centre in the garbage can on the far right side of the bar. "I quit" was all he said.

The bartender's eyes met mine once again as he declared incredulously, "He must really love you." With that, I received the confirmation I had hoped for. Jake was no doubt the man I was supposed to marry.

I thought how tenacious and strong-willed Jake was and wondered if he could truly pull it off and quit smoking right there on the spot. It became clear to me that once he set his mind to something, nothing and nobody could stop him. I thought how great it would be to have him by my side in life (only I had not thought of what it would be like to oppose his tenacity).

Since I would now be Jake's second wife, he let me know he did not want to go through all the technicalities and expenses of a wedding. "We'll elope and spend the money we would have spent on a wedding to buy a house," he reasoned. Though I personally wanted to have an official wedding, both he and the government seemed to agree that, within a matter of months, we would be common-law spouses, legally. Why go through the expense for something that was going to happen inevitably? I reasoned it made sense.

Five months after we first met, I was sitting on the edge of a hotel bed in Niagara Falls, the honeymoon capital of Canada. I looked across the room at him and he walked over to me and asked, "Are you ready?"

I simply nodded. Then he pulled the wedding band out of his pocket and slipped it onto my finger. "With this ring, I agree to stay with you as long as I'm happy," he declared.

My head shifted slightly as I processed what I had just heard (but I also thought, *perhaps he had a point*). Then I took out a gold ring, placed it on his finger and repeated, "With this ring, I agree to stay with you as long as I'm happy." Then we kissed and so it was: we were officially, yet unofficially married. Though not the fairytale wedding I had always dreamed of, I believed that was just the way life went, so I went with it.

"Let's go out and celebrate," Jake suggested. We did have a few things to celebrate, not only our new life together as husband and wife, but also that it was the day after my 21st birthday.

What just happened up there?

Seven years later, I found myself in a house full of children: our five year old son (who had blonde hair and blue eyes); our three year old daughter; and four foster children—three of which had been living with us for three years. It was a busy household but I loved it very much.

We owned and lived in a beautiful house that had four other apartments in it. My husband was busy working most of the time, so I was often home alone taking care of all six children.

I had become friends with one of our tenants, and one evening, when her own kids were visiting with their father, I invited her to join us for dinner. She sat there amongst our extended family across the table from Jake. We ate salad and then dinner.

Just as I prepared to serve dessert, my guest abruptly excused herself and went back downstairs.

In complete confusion, I immediately followed her. "What just happened up there?" I asked. She let me know my husband had insulted me thirty-three times during dinner and she had had enough. I was speechless. I did not know which shocked me more, that he had insulted me thirty-three times or that she had actually counted them.

I was confused, but I knew she was right. I knew that I did not want to live in a verbally abusive relationship but I feared being alone, not having a man in my life and becoming a single parent. I could not fathom how I would handle caring for this large family all by myself. Although I was not prepared to leave him after being together eight years, I was not prepared to continue being insulted and demeaned for the rest of my life. Not knowing what to do, I simply did nothing. Then something happened that I could not ignore.

Who put you in charge?

It was February 2, 1992. That day, we all went to church just as we had done many times before. The preacher's sermon that day was, "Who Put You in Charge?" After the service, we went out for lunch, and then headed for home.

That night, shortly after I crawled into bed, my husband came into the room and sat on the edge of his side of the bed. He sat there an unusually long time. I wondered what he was thinking about, but I chose not to ask him. Instead I closed my eyes and tried to go to sleep.

A short time later, I felt him shift into bed. Suddenly, without warning, Jake swiftly rolled me flat onto my back in the middle of the bed and straddled me, using all his weight and strength to pin me down. I could not get him off me. I was confused and afraid. He had never done anything like this before.

I looked into his eyes. They pierced directly through me, full of fury. Through clenched teeth, he spit out, "Who put you in charge?" He moved his strong hands up to my neck and began to squeeze, choking me. Though I was in shock, I was still able to utter a scream. Then he repeated, "Who put you in charge?" as his hands gripped my throat even more tightly. I reached up and felt his arms—they felt like tree trunks and every muscle was tense. He was not letting go. I was able to cry out with a few desperate screams.

I reached high, trying to push him away, but only the tips of my fingers could reach him. My nail etched into the side of his neck and blood shot out from the wound I had inflicted. The light shining behind him showed the blood spray out with such force that it splattered all over the night table next to the bed, the lampshade, and the wall behind it. Everything was so surreal, as though I was watching a scene from a horror movie. I looked around for a way to get him off me but he had me trapped in the middle of my bed, pinned down, with nothing to grip onto or grab hold of.

I was about to experience my own death.

I screamed even louder, hoping that one of the six children would get up — while also hoping they would not. I was amazed that I was even able to scream, considering he was strangling me.

Finally, he released one of his hands. I thought he would stop, but that hope was short-lived, as he quickly used that hand to cover my mouth. I gasped frantically for air. He realized he had failed to cover my nose, so he adjusted his grip, effectively covering my mouth and nose. Then he pressed down, hard.

My body went limp. I felt as if I was drowning, but for some reason I was not afraid. I did not see a bright light or darkness — everything was just gray. My eyes shut and refused to open. I was very tired and just wanted to drift off into a deep sleep. As I began surrendering to this feeling, the realization came over me that I was not about to drift into sleep—I was about to experience my own death.

I thought of my little ones who were sleeping in the next room. I imagined what their lives would be like if their mother was dead and their father was in jail for murdering her. At that moment, I knew I could not let this happen. I could do nothing more physically, for I was incapable of moving, unable to speak, and no longer able to breathe. I did the only thing I could think to do... I prayed silently, "God help!"

At that very instant, there was a knock at our back door. It was as though God had been waiting for my request. At the sound of the knock, my husband leapt off me, as though the person standing on the other side of the door could see what he was doing. I gasped for air and immediately got off the bed.

The irony of the very first words.

I followed him out to see who had come to answer my prayer. It was one of our tenants from two floors down—a woman I barely knew. She asked my husband if everything was all right. He replied that everything was fine. Then I stepped into her sight. She gasped, and then covered her mouth with her hand in shock. I had no idea what she saw, but I could taste blood in my mouth. I felt my lip and realized it had been split open by the pressure of his hand pressing on my mouth. She looked at my neck and nervously queried, "Were you just strangled with a rope?" Embarrassed I lowered my head and tried to cover myself with my hands. "And what happened to your eyes?" she asked, remarking that they were completely bloodshot, and that my eyelids were speckled with red. I began to cry, the shock of what I had just suffered engulfed me.

She invited me to sleep on her sofa, but I feared for the safety of my son and daughter. I was unsure how angry he still might be, so I thought it best to stay with them and protect them by sleeping in their room with them. "Thank you, but I'll just stay up here with my kids," I told her.

"Are you sure?" she insisted.

"Yeah, I'll be fine. I need to make sure they are safe. I'll just sleep in their bed tonight. We'll be okay," I tried to reassure her—and myself.

"Promise me you'll call the police tomorrow."

"I will," I promised. With that, she walked past me and went back downstairs. Just two short flights, the stairs had never seemed that far down before. The farther she went down them, the more alone I felt.

I walked quickly toward my children's room in hopes that I would not meet my husband in the narrow hallway on my way there. I raced past the washroom, not daring to stop for fear that the longer I took, the greater the opportunity he would have to find me. I entered their room quickly and shut the door behind me.

They had a queen-sized bed I had set sideways so that each would have more room to sleep side by side. Being careful not to wake them, I crawled up onto the mattress between them and nestled the blankets around me. I stared at the lights floating onto the ceiling with each passing car outside until I was certain he would not try to find me. Only then was I finally able to drift into sleep. Resting between my own son and daughter, I felt both protective and protected.

My last thought before sleep was the irony of the very first words I had spoken to him years prior, when he had approached me asking for a knife. I had replied, "As long as you promise not to kill anyone."

Thirty seconds away.

The following morning, I could hear Jake shoveling the snow, so I quickly went into our room, dressed and left out the back door. Instead of calling the police, I went directly to my doctor. After examining me, she told me the broken capillaries on my eyelids and around my eyes were telltale signs of the final stages of strangulation. I had been about thirty seconds away from death. It was then that the reality and severity of what had just happened hit me fully.

With this confirmation, I called the police and met them at my home. They arrested Jake. I then took a copy of the medical report and a confirmation of the police report and went to the courthouse. Within hours, I was able to see the judge, who granted me sole custody of both of my children, and a restraining order against Jake. I was shocked to learn that, regardless of the restraining order, according to Canadian law, he would still have permission to spend time with his children. The fact that he had nearly killed me made no difference. Essentially, they were letting me know that I had no legal recourse. I feared for the safety and well-being of those two while in his care.

I was also afraid for me. Along with the fear of raising my family alone and the fear of death, I was also afraid of men in general. What I had always admired about men—their strength, their stature, their masculinity—I was afraid of all of it now.

At the time, I thought that the situation was settled, resolved, and that I would no longer have to deal with it. Little did I know, this incident was only the beginning of things that were about to unravel out of my control.

Chapter Three

Residual Effects

My very core ached with pain.

One month after the assault, one of the foster kid's social workers came by for her usual scheduled weekly visit. She asked, almost in passing, where my husband was because she had not seen him around over the past few weeks.

Tears uncontrollably poured down my face, both ashamed and in pain, I admitted, "He violently assaulted me, so we are separated. He doesn't live here anymore." She sat quietly and allowed me to compose myself.

"Where do you plan to live?" she asked with concern. I poured out my thoughts and concerns to her as if she was a friend. I let her know that I was not sure, since my now, ex-husband, had sent letters to all the tenants instructing them to pay rent directly to him. He was not paying our mortgage with those funds, but was keeping the money for himself. I knew that because of his actions, I would soon be in arrears, gravely so, and the bank would repossess my home.

As she listened intently to what I had to say, her face showed a look of dismay. The next words she spoke took my breath away, "The foster kids need to be removed immediately." She had no choice in light of what I had just said.

At the full realization of what I had just divulged, I gasped and covered my mouth as if to stop myself from saying anything more—though there was nothing left to say. I desperately wanted to retract all that I had said, but instead pleaded, "Please don't take them away. They are my family. They are my children's family. Please let them stay."

"I can't," she flatly stated. She really did have no choice. New tears formed and followed the path of the previous ones. As she saw herself out, she turned around to face me one final time, "Someone will come by to pick them up and their belongings before 9 p.m. tonight." My very core ached with pain. I had loved and cared for three of the four almost as long as I had my own.

By 7:30 that night, they took away the first child. By 8:15, the rest were gone.

That tingling, numbing sensation.

I knew I needed to move forward with my life. Otherwise, the pain would paralyze me.

About a week later, I was in the local library when I found a pamphlet in the front foyer that read, *"Ladies night every Saturday night."* It was not very descriptive but sounded interesting, so I picked it up and tucked it away in my purse.

A few weeks later, my children were set to visit with their father. I dreaded the thought of being home alone for yet another weekend. I was still trying to get used to the silence of the four-bedroom house that once housed so many youngster's voices and peals of laughter.

Rather than face another Saturday night home alone, I decided to check out this "Ladies night." I did not know what to wear, since I had not gone out to bars much. I was married so young that I had never gotten into the party scene, drinking, and going to bars.

I assumed ladies night would be a safe place for me to go, both because I found this information in a public library, and because there would be a lot of woman there that I could hang out with. I would not be exposed to any men and thus risked no harassment.

I finally arrived at a dilapidated part of the downtown Toronto core. I had never been in that part of Toronto before but that is where the address had led me. I entered through the blackened front door and walked down the concrete staircase into the dimly lit basement. The blaring music drew me in.

As I walked in, my eyes scanned the room. I saw a sea of women. There were so many, the occasional male I spotted seemed oddly out of place. I wondered how many of the women there were afraid of men as I was. I wondered if there was any other reason why they might be here. Shyly, I walked up to the bar to order a soda, to have something to hold in my hands.

A woman came up to me and introduced herself, "Hi, I'm Cathy." Then she asked if I had ever been there before. I told her it was my first time. We just stood together, silently watching the crowd of women dancing together in a way I had only seen straight couples dance previously. I was mesmerized, bewildered... and intrigued. As I watched them dancing, I thought how bizarre a scene it was.

I still wasn't altogether clear on what was going on until Cathy leaned over to me and confirmed what I suspected, "Isn't this a great lesbian nightclub?"

I was speechless.

I thought it was not possible for two women to be together. I always thought being homosexual was wrong, so I had never given it a second consideration. I thought back to all the pretty girls I knew in high school. Oddly, it had never even crossed my mind to make a pass at any of them, nor did any of them ever make a pass at me.

Suddenly Cathy, who was still standing next to me, touched my cheek. As I turned to look her way, the two women next to us lip-locked in an intense, passionate kiss. Cathy saw them, then turned to me and said, "I would really like to kiss *you*!"

The feeling that immediately took over my body was an overwhelming, intense tingling, yet numbing sensation. It was as if a thousand butterflies fluttered in my stomach. I was so confused. At first, I was tempted to leave immediately and never return. That temptation was fleeting, replaced by a completely consuming sensation. I chose to stay and explore the new feeling. I allowed it all to unfold, curious to see where it would lead.

Like a drug.

Nothing came of her request as I shyly turned away and then left shortly thereafter. Over the weeks, however, I kept thinking about Cathy. I wondered about that deep feeling I had experienced. Why had my legs gone numb? Why did it feel like butterflies, only more intense? I knew I needed to go back.

It was weeks before I would return. In the meantime, I kept busy caring for my small family and did all that was required of me, though my mind was on what I had experienced that night and going back. Many thoughts rushed through my mind: that it would be okay for me to dance with another woman, hold hands with her, be close to her, get to know her, and possibly even kiss her... to partake in the "forbidden fruit." I was amazed that it appeared to be totally acceptable. At least that is what the room full of strangers in the women's nightclub led me to believe.

Finally, I had the opportunity to go to the nightclub a second time, so I dressed up and headed out. This time, it felt a bit more familiar.

I searched through the crowd of women to find Cathy. I was desperate to find her since that tingling sensation came back to me every time I thought of her. I searched everywhere but she was nowhere to be found. My heart sank. I felt like I did back in high school when I was heartbroken after my first love. This surprised me. I barely knew this woman, and she didn't know me at all. I wondered why I was feeling this way. Not able to shake it, I decided to go to the bar to get a drink. Not knowing what to have I ordered something fruity that came with a Maraschino cherry.

As I waited to be served a tall sporty looking woman came up to me. "You don't look like a lesbian, are you?" She questioned.

I opened my mouth to speak but nothing came out. I wondered what she meant. I did not realize lesbians looked a certain way. Not knowing how to respond, I raised my glass and took a huge gulp. Not accustomed to drinking alcohol I found myself drinking it like water. Before I knew it my cocktail was gone.

"Can I buy you another one?" asked this sporty woman.

Without much hesitation I nodded my head. As she handed me a new drink, her hand touched mine. That tingling sensation returned. I was now captivated by my own feelings. Before I had the chance to explore them further, her friends came by and she was gone.

It was now late, so I left.

I needed to settle this feeling I was getting with these woman. So a few weeks later, I headed out to go there a third time but found, to my dismay; the nightclub was shut down and no longer there. I was devastated and had no idea where it had gone. I knew no other place to go to find the women I had met there. There I stood alone, completely dressed up, in the run-down side of town, on a cold rainy night. I had just discovered this amazing underworld, only to have it torn away from me. I had to find these women again.

I just needed to learn more about this homosexual lifestyle. The sensation I felt when I was with these women was like a drug. I wanted more and needed more. It was an entirely new world and I desperately sought to experience it.

She had a girlfriend.

The bank repossessed the large house that Jake, our children and I had once called home. We left all those memories behind as my children and I moved into a townhouse. In June of that same year, my son turned six. Ambitiously, I decided to invite his entire class over for his birthday party. One by one, the parents came over to drop off their child directly from school due my son's birthday falling on the last day of school.

I soon had my hands full with eighteen 6-year olds. I was shocked, but grateful when one of the moms offered to stay and help out, and gratefully accepted her offer. Everyone had a wonderful time.

The party came off without a hitch and the helpful mom stayed until the very last parent picked up her child. Afterwards, my son and her son continued to play and we both sat down at the kitchen table and talked, over a pot of hot tea.

Her name was Tanita and she was a beautiful native woman, with long black hair, brown eyes, and a beautiful smile. We shared our stories. Like Jake and I, she and her husband had broken up not too long ago, about six months before us.

She had two sons and shared with me that her boys lived primarily with their father, that he had sole custody. Judgment immediately arose in me as I wondered what type of mother would agree to such a thing. She let me know she was okay with this arrangement because it allowed her to live the life-style she wanted. Now I was intrigued. What type of lifestyle was she referring to?

She reached over and held my hand in hers. "I used to have long nails too," she commented as she noticed mine. She mentioned that long nails were not conducive to her current life-style. I hesitantly asked her what she meant.

"I have a girlfriend," she boldly stated.

"You're a lesbian?" I immediately questioned for clarification.

"We prefer being called gay women, non straight or same-sex. Being called homosexual seems a bit too formal, but yeah, I'm a lesbian." She declared.

I was shocked. Here was this beautiful woman, standing in the middle of my kitchen, telling me that she is gay—after leaving her husband of six years. It was like an answer to my prayer (well, I had not actually prayed to have a gay woman in my house, but here she was anyway), and I was caught up in the moment.

I wondered how she could be so confident to declare such a thing. After all, I still could not imagine it was real—at least not real outside of the nightclub. I was shocked. I secretly wished that if I chose to pursue this avenue, that I too could one day be confident and declarative as she was. For now I was receiving exactly what I had hoped for, a way back into the homosexual world I knew so little about.

I told her of my brief encounter at the women's nightclub. I told her about the incredible, numbing sensation I had experienced. She nodded then added how wonderful it felt, like intense butterflies, which echoed my own experience. "It looks like you belong on our team," she told me with a sparkle in her eyes and a grin that captivated her face.

Tanita completely drew me in. It had only been five months since my "ex" and I separated. Here I was, talking to a woman, a mom just like me, who was interested in women—just like me. Only she was so open about it all—just like I one day hoped to be. I was amazed at how quickly the two of us bonded. The frightening reality was she was still a total stranger.

Turning into a convertible.

Soon, Tanita and I became friends. I made very few friends during the years Jake and I had been together, simply because Toronto was home to his friends and family, not mine. Besides, during the years we had been together, I spent most of my time caring for our family of eight. I had not thought it important to gain friendships, so I welcomed Tanita as a new friend. I longed to learn more about what the homosexual lifestyle had to offer.

She introduced me to her girlfriend, Sammy (full name Samantha), along with their group of friends. When I first walked into Sammy's house, it appeared to be a typical two-bedroom bungalow, only it seemed more like a guy's hangout than a woman's home. There were cases of empty beer bottles stacked in the corner of the kitchen. A calendar of partially naked women hung on the wall next to the telephone. An ash-tray overflowing with cigarette butts rested in the middle of the two-seater kitchen table. A sink full of empty coffee mugs lay in the sink.

In the adjoining living room was an electric guitar perched on a stand in the corner. The stereo blared. Cigarette smoke clouded the air. The room was filled with women—all laughing and making jokes, listening to music they all apparently knew the words to, but that I had never heard before.

Tanita quickly introduced me to the six women sitting around the room. She proceeded to introduce everyone in a way that struck me as bizarre, pointing to each as she called their names: "This is Lynn, who used to date Trish, who is now with Katie, also Trish's old partner. There is Trish, who is now dating Rachel, who used to date Katie. Oh, and there are Claudia and Paula-Jean—PJ for short—who we found hanging out, and making out at the club last Saturday night."

The look on my face got them all laughing. "Well, that's how it is in the gay community," Tanita informed me. "It's small, so everybody knows everybody. But..." she continued intentionally, "when you find the right one, you'll be happier than you've ever been before." She reached her arms around Sammy and leaned in for a passionate kiss, causing all the other women to cheer. Almost reading my mind, Tanita responded to my apparent look of shock and stated, "It's okay, you'll get used to it." Then she let me know that soon I would find it strange to see a man and a woman—"breeders" as she called them—kissing. The rest of the women backed her up, in agreement. "Stick with us, we'll turn you into a convertible," she laughed clarifying they would assist in converting me from a heterosexual to a homosexual.

Altering every possible thought.

I wanted to learn everything there was to learn in order to feel like I belonged and fit in. As strange as these thoughts seemed at first, I decided I was open to the prospect of having my thoughts shift in line with theirs. With that, I willingly began my gay-makeover conversion process.

I was introduced to gay music (either the artist was gay, or the lyrics were gay-friendly), the appropriate way to dress— feminine but not too "girly," how to walk, dance, think, behave, what to believe, where to hang out, even what types of drinks I should order—the ones with Maraschino cherries on top were too girly so not a good choice, I was informed. They laughed while they shared this information with me as though they knew what I would be thinking because they had already been in this same situation. "It's okay, just hang out with us and you'll soon get the hang of it," they promised.

They let me know I would soon have well tuned "gaydar" which was just like radar but for gay detection. With gaydar, I would be able to spot a gay person anywhere, and they would be able to spot me. I was curious to find out if this actually worked.

A common topic of discussion was about who was out, who was not, how long they had been out, and who they were out to (just their closest friends, people at work, or to everyone they met or ran into). They applauded and cheered for anyone who had recently come out.

They worked tirelessly at helping me alter and convert my mind until I began believing that heterosexuality was not normal for everyone, especially those who had gay feelings or tendencies. Homosexuality made so much sense, they asserted, because "a woman knows what a woman wants" and "a man knows what a man wants."

They believed that the heterosexual lifestyle was simply for those who were too scared or insecure to break out of that old fashioned mold to experience the homosexual relationship that would prove to be exactly what they had been missing all their lives.

My gay friends assisted me in altering every possible thought I had about the opposite sex. Eventually, I began to see what they saw, feel what they felt, and did what they were doing.

It's just part of the initiation process.

A year passed since I met Tanita and it was now again the end of June. I was at Sammy's place on a Friday night while she and Tanita were busy tidying up, getting ready to greet one of Sammy's old friends. When I asked who it was, I was told, "the lead singer of a band."

I gave this no more thought and just made myself at home, just as I had been told to do, ever since my first visit. I sat down on the sofa and put their black and white cat on my lap. At first, they had named the cat Jackie, but later discovered that "she" was a "he" and promptly renamed him Jack. Thus, he became what they described as the, "only male in the house." Tanita let me know this cat also provided her comfort since her own boys were rarely around.

As I sat stroking Jack, there was a knock at the front door. When they opened up the door, I was amazed to learn who their guest was. It was none other than the female lead singer of the all-female band with that obvious Hollywood name that had brought me to Toronto nearly ten years prior. She had come down to partake in the Gay Pride festivities being held this weekend.

I leaned into Tanita and shared my previous encounter with this singer. "Didn't you realize it was a gay band?" she questioned almost laughing at me. I had not.

"See?" she said. "It's fate! You're clearly gay!" she broadcasted, without hesitation. "So why don't you just come out?" she asked while reaching over to pick Jack up.

I knew I still wasn't ready to commit.

The other women overheard our conversation and spoke out in agreement. They reasoned I would eventually have to do it sometime, promising me I would feel so much better when I no longer had to hide my true self.

They encouraged me to simply come out to everyone: my friends, family, son, daughter, their school, my job. They predicted the responses and reactions I was likely to elicit during my coming out process. They even coached me with responses I could give to counterbalance any disapproval I received.

Although it appeared every possible scenario was covered, I was still afraid I was not yet ready, so I hoped instead, nobody would find out.

"Why are you making this more difficult than it needs to be?" Tanita asked. "We all had to do it," she reasoned. Although it would be a bit tough at first, it eventually would get easier she promised. "It's just part of the initiation process," she justified.

Then one of the women let me know it would be much better for me to come out than to be "outted" or "found out." She, herself had been found out and explained how she felt completely violated by the person who outted her—who had taken the liberty of stripping something precious, private and personal away from her that she had not condoned, and could not recover back. She told me it had been a horribly violating experience. She recommended I would be better off just to expose and out myself.

A look of shock and bewilderment came over my face.

"Well if you can't come out of the closet, at least come out to play," Tanita lightened the mood and invited me to join in on the festivities.

My curiosity compelled me to go. Years prior, I had glimpsed the front page of the newspaper which had captured various questionable photographs of the Gay Pride Parade including half-naked people dancing on floats.

"It's a lot of fun," Tanita promised.

Not knowing what else to expect, but curious, I agreed to join them. We all loaded into Sammy's car. She turned on some gay-friendly tunes and we proceeded into the downtown Toronto core.

Trying to be accepted as being 'normal'?

By the time we reached Church Street, there was nowhere to park. The streets had been barricaded off and everyone was allowed to walk freely down the center of the roads. Tanita and Sammy walked into a corner store and bought some gum, cigarettes, and a lighter with a pink upside down triangle displayed on it. Then she bought a rainbow-colored flag. "You want one?" she offered, letting me know they were both homosexual symbols. I declined. She chuckled at me, reached over for Sammy's hand and we all joined the crowd.

There were booths with people selling everything imaginable. One woman selling jewelry captured my attention when Tanita ran up to her, hugged her, then jokingly told her to put some clothes on—the woman was topless. I was astounded to see the sights: men walking around with chaps on that revealed their bare backsides, others in dog collars being led by their partner, others in drag, bare breasted women with sparkles and designs painted all over them.

It was as though I had entered an alternate universe. "Aren't these people trying to be accepted as being 'normal' by society?" I asked Tanita. She simply smiled, then eluded the question by letting me know it would be a great place to pick up someone.

We made our way to where the parade was passing and stood there being squirted with water guns as the floats passed by. Banners advertised various groups and organizations that supported gay rights. A banner preceding a man in Preacher attired captured my attention. The banner advertised the name of a church. A moment later, I picked up a business card flung in my direction. It bore the same church name and address as the banner. "What you got there?" Tanita asked. I showed her. "See, even God wants you to be gay," she joked before focusing her attention back on Sammy. I slipped the business card into my wallet.

Before the night was through.

A few days after the parade, Tanita let me know that she and Sammy had split up. I seemed more upset at the news than she did. "What happened?" I questioned.

"We each met someone new at the Gay Pride Parade," she said.

"How did that happen?" I was curious since I had seen them holding hands for most of the day. It was someone she had met in the washroom. In fact, while she had been in the washroom, someone had approached Sammy as she sat outside waiting for Tanita to return. They had hit it off as well.

I was shocked. She simply brushed it off and let me know things like this happened all the time. She said that people who were couples already were particularly attractive and alluring than those who were alone. She looked at me and said, "That's probably why you didn't find anyone, because you were alone."

Then Tanita informed me that the woman she had met was currently in a relationship but wanted out. She had invited Tanita and me to come over to their place to intervene. When I questioned Tanita about her intentions prior to arriving at the couple's house, she simply stated if I were "more gay," her plan would work better.

"More gay?" I questioned.

In response, she shared a scenario.

"Let's say Jane and Joanne are a couple and Katie and Karen are a couple. If Jane and Joanne are having a disagreement and Katie and Karen come over to visit, then Jane might consider having an affair with either Katie or Karen. Joanne might also be considering the same thing for herself. Females share a tight bond with other females, so if Jane goes outside for a cigarette and Katie decides to join her, then within minutes, Jane could reveal that she and her partner are going through difficulties, consequently turning to Katie for comfort. As a result, an affair is likely.

"In the meantime, Joanne and Karen have been sitting together inside and are also having a conversation and possibly reaching a point of connection. By the time the evening is over, the partners have switched. That is why I wish you were 'more gay,' so you could attract the other partner."

"You have got to be kidding," I said. "I can't imagine anyone bonding that quickly."

She replied, "I know. I didn't believe it until I first saw it too, but trust me, it can and does happen this quickly. That's what happened to Sammy and me. Besides, how do you think all those other women ended up together who used to date each other?"

She explained to me that since I had not yet experienced a committed homosexual relationship, I could not possibly understand the depth and electrifying magnetic attraction that comes out of that type of relationship. I was shocked, but agreed to go along with her anyway.

That night, I sat in the living room while her plan manifested before my very eyes. Before the night was through, she felt emotionally connected with the woman she was attracted to and they were planning to meet the next night. Soon afterwards, they became involved in a relationship.

This entire experience was so unique to me. I was accustomed to the dynamics of heterosexual relationships where, given the same circumstances, there is only one option for each of the four people in the room. In a gay relationship, there are double the options and double the people involved, effectively quadrupling the possibilities.

Knowing this, I still chose to embrace the homosexual lifestyle. I believed and hoped that one day I would find the woman of my dreams and our relationship would be different than all the rest—that ours would surpass all this emotional and intimate tug and pull. Our relationship would last forever!

Does God make mistakes?

I pulled out the church business card I had stuffed into my wallet at the Gay Pride Parade. I knew I could not fully commit to my new lifestyle until I found a church to support my new-found beliefs. Although I had gone through periods in my life when I wanted to reject religion and spirituality as a whole because I felt it would stop me from truly enjoying my life and living it "my way," I still needed assurance that I was not going to end up in hell.

I chose first to walk into a Catholic church to question a priest about the possible ramifications of choosing to live a homosexual lifestyle. He answered that if I did, I would not "inherit or have any share in the kingdom of God." I was not sure what that meant and decided that since I was not sure, it could not be that important. After all, he had not told me I would go to hell and that was all I believed I needed to know.

The following Sunday, I walked into the gay church. I was astounded, surrounded by the quaint old architecture and stained-glass windows. It was full of character. Wooden benches arranged in a semi-circle, faced the altar from the front row all the way to the back. A big wooden cross was at the front, resting over the organ pipes. Red velvet curtains adorned either side. I noticed a small quiet room to the back of the church on the left, and an old wooden staircase leading to the upper balcony, which also faced the pulpit in a semi-circular position.

I settled on finding a seat near the back of the church on the main floor. The organist began to play. Then a singer approached the front of the sanctuary and began to sing. When the song was finished, the gay preacher came to the front and welcomed us all for being there. I recognized him from the float in the parade.

That day, something moved within me. I sat there and tears began streaming down my face uncontrollably. I looked around, searching frantically for something to wipe away the tears, when the person next to me handed me a box of tissues.

"Are you new here?" she asked me. I nodded yes. "You'll be alright," she consoled. "Most of us cried when we first entered this church." Then she smiled and handed me another tissue. Although I had not asked her name, her small gesture of kindness made me feel welcome.

The preacher stood at the front, opened up the Bible, and began to speak. He quoted scripture, shared verses and stories, and preached a sermon. Before he finished speaking, he reminded us that God loves and accepts all people, regardless of their sexual orientation. He assured us that none of us was a mistake—straight, homosexual or otherwise—because God does not make mistakes. He taught that we are all created equal, and that we should be proud of who we were.

Through his teaching and preaching, he assured us that if anyone outside the four walls of the church questioned our integrity or our choice to live our lives as homosexuals, we could rest assured that we were simply living our lives the way we were created to live it. He assured us that in time, society would eventually catch up and accept us for who we are. This verification imparted a sense of peace and comfort to me.

I committed to attending this church as often as possiblc. It gave me greater strength to face every new challenge. It helped me to become proud of my new lifestyle. I could not wait to go to church every Sunday morning because I knew it would fill me again with encouraging words about being a homosexual, and I would be surrounded by others of like mind. We celebrated our beliefs and similarities as well as our uniqueness and individuality.

I turned to this church for truth, comfort and guidance. This church even held classes that taught acceptance of homosexuals. I never did attend one of those classes, but just knowing they were available was reassuring.

I believed I had finally found where I belonged, in a community of others who also experienced this wonderful sense of belonging. Having found this gay church made me feel good about my new lifestyle.

I also felt good letting the "straight" people know that I went to church every Sunday morning with my two children. I did not feel the need to go into detail about what type of church it was, especially with anyone who was still not aware of my sexual orientation. This allowed me to appear not only normal but exceptional. I appeared to be a wonderful single mom who brought her two well-behaved children to church every Sunday. Clearly, I had thought this whole thing through. Being a homosexual was my new lifestyle. All I had to do was alter my complete existence and have the new existence fall in line with a simile of the old one that I used to have.

The more I hung out with my gay friends, and the more I went to the gay church, the more confident I became.

This became a juicy piece of gossip.

After several months of attending this church, I became fully committed to moving forward with my life by coming out. I would never have had the courage to take the huge step, had it not been for this perfect, totally accepting church.

It had given me a sense of preeminence and the courage to do whatever I needed to do in order to get my whole life in line with this new reality—this world of the non-straight life. I was accepting this lifestyle for myself and I was on a mission to let others know about it as well. I believed when I took this bold step, I would be free from my fear of judgment because I was not alone. I now had the support of an entire gay community to justify my new lifestyle choice and decision. This was the real me. I was gay, proud, not-straight, and now I was coming out.

I made the decision that I would simply tell everyone about my new life—I would hold it back from no one.

First, I let my older sister know. Though after witnessing my behavior over the previous year, she said to me, "I was wondering when you would finally admit it." This clearly gave me the confidence I needed to continue what I needed to do.

Then I inadvertently let my mother know because it slipped out at Christmas when my sister and I were talking about my newest love and my mother walked in on us. She asked what we were discussing. In all of my stuttering, muttering and hesitation, my older sister simply blurted out, "Oh, for crying out loud mom, she's a lesbian!"

My mom's mouth dropped and all she could muster to say was, "No, no, no, no, no!" and began to cry.

My sister quickly changed the topic and nothing more was said. Although my mother was clearly distraught, she did not reject or turn away from me.

Then I let my father know. He was supportive of me because I am his daughter and he is a wonderful man who would support me in anything I chose to do.

My younger sister had lived only in small towns—the one we grew up in and then another—so she was pretty sheltered. Surprisingly, when I told her, she was non-judgmental, in fact seemed to be in awe and amazement.

Then, in order to secure my place in the community, I let my children's school know of my sexual orientation by informing the teachers and the Principal.

Then I let the government know when one of those polling surveys came around, asking if the members of the household were single, married, divorced or common-law. I wrote next to it in big bold letters: SAME-SEX RELATIONSHIP! (Later

I discovered these polling surveys were not read by some big parliament man in downtown Ottawa, but by people in my community—including parents of those who attended school with mine.) This became a juicy piece of gossip. It also became the source of whispers I overheard the next time I dropped my children off for school. So at that point, I came to terms with the fact that anyone who had not known about my lifestyle would know soon enough.

I embraced and accepted my newfound lifestyle and allowed it to become my reality in every avenue of my life.

I had finally unofficially and officially become an unquestionably undeniably full-fledged homosexual and proudly labeled myself as such. I became the lesbian sister, the gay mom, the homosexual neighbor. I was numerous things preceded by the words lesbian, gay, same-sex, non-straight, or homosexual.

I finally felt free to be me. I could not wait to see what wonderful journeys this new lifestyle had in store for me. I could not wait to find that special woman in my life, so I could finally have a wonderful, perfect, effortless relationship, and finally live out the life of my dreams.

Chapter Four

Chosen Lifestyle Lived Out

Alternative to what?

It was August 12, 1998. I was in the downtown gay core with my friends, when out of the corner of my eye, I noticed a beautiful woman leaning up against the bar. She was one of those ladies that did not look like a "typical" gay woman.

I knew I needed to meet her. Although I had been in the gay scene for six years now, I had not made many passes at other woman so I did not know what to say or how to approach her. All I knew was that I could not let this opportunity go by.

After a few more songs and after some much needed courage, I casually made my way over to the bar where she was standing. Before long, I made a lame pass at her. I had little time to assess my pass or to attempt another one because her question back to me caught me off guard. "What are you thinking about?" she asked.

"I was just thinking I would like to kiss you," I answered in brutal honesty. The reality of which completely shocked me.

"So kiss me," she replied.

Although I was astounded at myself for what I had just said, her response led me to believe it was acceptable. Not knowing what else to say or do, I leaned over and kissed her.

I could not believe what I had just said and done, nor understand where my boldness and forwardness came from. I would have never accepted this forwardness from any man in my past, but somehow, while in this room, within this environment, surrounded by this atmosphere—in spite of my own values, morals, and ethics—I had allowed myself to become this person I barely recognized.

When I tried to apologize for being so forward, she stopped me and told me it was nice to see that I was so brave and openly gay, out, and proud.

It paused to think of what had just transpired and realized I had two options—to actually be brave and proud, or to be ashamed. I decided to be proud.

It was as though this homosexual lifestyle altered my entire sense of reality. It not only altered my thought process and my opinions, it led me to believe I could reinvent myself. It emboldened me to believe I had the power to say absolutely anything I wanted to say, and do anything I wanted to do, whenever and wherever I wanted to do it. It was an existence where I could become anyone I dared to be, follow my feelings and be bold and proud of it!

I came to realize that living this alternative lifestyle was like living in an alternative world, full of alternative beliefs and truths, filled with alternative goals and aspirations, in an alternative dimension of reality.

I was so busy trying to figure out all my new alternatives, I never paused to ask myself the question, "Alternative to what?"

Things were about to decline.

Months passed, and as they did, I grew closer and closer to this wonderful woman named Zoe that I met at the bar that "fateful" night. I was extremely happy. Things happened in our relationship that made me believe she was "the one." As our relationship grew, the desire to spend more time together also grew. As the first year of our relationship unfolded, we realized we had so many things in common that, for many reasons, we had what it would take to create a strong lifelong relationship. I became madly, deeply, truly in love with her. I had finally found the one I believed was my soul mate, the one I had been waiting for all my life.

We went to the gay church regularly, Zoe and I, and my son and daughter. We would worship together and sing together. Many times, people in the congregation would come up to us after services to tell us we looked like the perfect couple, even the perfect family.

From the outside, our life appeared to be glorious—but what was happening behind the scenes was anything but glorious. I did not realize it then, but my life, and everything that mattered to me, was about to decline into a downward spiral, and out of my control.

It was utter maddness.

When I first met Zoe, Jake and I had been separated for six years. I had maintained sole custody of the children and had a restraining order against him. At the time of our separation, I was young and just wanted out. I did not think things through.

So over the initial four months following the assault, along with the other traumas I faced at the time, I gave him every material thing I could in the hope that it would resolve the situation quickly. I signed everything over to him: the houses we owned, the furniture, the van, my rights to his pension plan, alimony payments—absolutely everything, except for my two children. This was all I wanted and asked for. Once he signed the paperwork and received everything I had willingly allowed him to have, he proceeded to initiate court proceedings to take away from me the only thing I had asked for and truly cherished—my son and daughter.

He proceeded to drag me into court approximately every six months since our separation. This caused me to suffer many sleepless nights filled with worry, dread and confusion. I had no idea about my future or the future of my children and it caused me great anxiety. Because I could not sleep, I often felt exhausted during the day, and wished it were night so I could rest. Then night would come and I'd wish it was day because I had so many phone calls to make and people to talk to that I did not seem to have the time or strength to deal with the previous day, due to caring for the children. I continued to fight to keep them, but year after year, he fought to take them away from me. It was utter madness.

My children were suffering.

By the time Zoe and I had been together a little over a year, and become more serious, things changed for the worse. For years, I had successfully maintained sole custody in spite of desperate attempts by my ex to discredit me. Finally, he changed his angle and successfully urged the two of them to fill out legal documentation that let the court know their reasons for wanting to live with him rather than with me. I later learned he had promised them everything they wanted to hear—no chores, no responsibility, no bed time, all the TV watching they wanted, pets, an allowance, and all the candy they could eat.

These poor children were emotionally torn and my ex was doing everything in his power to take them away from me. His behavior was so aggressive that it even stumped the lawyers. They were clearly dazed and confused about his insistence and refusal to settle for anything less than taking my children completely away from me. They simply could not understand the measures he had been willing to go to which were clearly emotionally damaging to these little ones. I had seen this side of him before, when he had quit smoking. I knew then that he was tenacious; now I was experiencing the full force of that tenacity coming up against me. Worst yet, these innocent two were the ones who were suffering.

My son, who was 11, finally pleaded for me to make it all stop. I knew for their sake, I needed to do whatever was necessary in order to stop this insanity. I turned to my lawyer who could not help, the courts could not help, the police, social workers and counselors were unable to do anything. There was only one thing left that I could do. I would need to release my children and allow them to go with their father, who was causing this insanity in their lives to begin with.

After six excruciating years of court custody battles, without further recourse, in the greatest agony I could possibly imagine, I signed sole custody over to my ex. Having signed away my legal rights, my children were taken away from me. There I stood, in a merciless courtroom environment, having just signed this heartless document, with no one but my same-sex partner there to comfort me. I never felt so empty, worthless, humiliated, damaged, torn, broken, or alone in all my life.

I tried desperately to maintain regular contact with my son and daughter, but we now lived two hours apart. In addition, they would often cancel our weekend get-togethers for one reason or another. I wanted desperately to spend more time with them but also felt if I pushed it that they might become resentful, considering they would have to leave their friends during their weekends to spend time alone with Zoe and me. I accepted their cancellations and tried to make the best of the situation, in spite of the pain I was feeling.

I felt damaged beyond repair, as if a part of me was missing. I felt like an unfit and undeserving parent, as if I was being punished. I tried desperately to maintain decorum at all times, but when the subject would turn to my children, I would break into tears every time, no matter where I was or what the circumstances were. Zoe was acutely aware of my sensitivity and would quickly change the subject when it was raised. She was my strength and I leaned on her for support.

We are gathered here today.

Zoe and I continued to rely on each other and consequently, our relationship grew stronger. It was now spring 2000. We headed to Niagara Falls for a weekend getaway. After we arrived and found a place to park, we walked towards the falls embracing the cool mist that is forever floating above that area. It was crisp and refreshing and both Zoe and I were enjoying the moment. Suddenly, to my surprise, Zoe reached inside her pocket and turned to face me. On bended knee, she presented me with an engagement ring and asked me to marry her. I was ecstatic.

I had proposed to her a week prior, presenting her with a replica of the same ring in the bottom of a champagne glass. She agreed to marry me. Now we had both experienced becoming engaged to one another. I never thought I would be fortunate enough to find a woman I loved so much, who loved me equally in return.

As soon as we returned from the weekend, we made an appointment to meet with the gay preacher. He let us know that he would perform a "Holy Union," since same-sex marriage was not legal, but that the paperwork we would sign were actual legal marriage certificates. When same-sex marriage became legal, he would submit them on our behalf and we would automatically become legally married in the eyes of the law.

Although I had been married, common-law, I had never walked down the aisle in a white wedding gown. This experience was going to be a first for both Zoe and me. We were both excited.

We knew the date to choose, August 12, 2000, the exact date of our first meeting two years prior. We both chose to wear a long white wedding dress, and have floral arrangements of simply white on white. We went in search of the perfect reception hall and found it, booked it, booked a white limousine, made a guest list, selected the dinner, found the perfect invitations, chose the perfect wedding song, and hired a DJ for the reception. As was customary, we booked a honeymoon in Jamaica.

I chose my older sister as my Maid of Honor, and Zoe chose her cousin as hers. Our wedding party would consist of the two of them plus both of my children.

As the day drew nearer, we both hoped our mothers would attend. While they did not know each other, they were both equally against us going through with marriage.

Finally, the day arrived. My father led me into the sanctuary of the church and Zoe met me at the altar, escorted by her brother. Neither of our mothers was in attendance.

We stood beside each other at the front of the church. The gay preacher welcomed us then began to preside, "We are gathered here today in the witness of family, and friends, and in the presence of God…"

We said our vows to one another, exchanged rings, signed the documents, and by the end of the service we had become wife and wife.

"I am your Lady, you are my Man…"

I had often heard of things going wrong at weddings, but what we encountered was more than what most would consider normal.

On the morning of our wedding, I went to pick up the bridal bouquets and flowers, but the florist had lost our order and they were not ready. They had to scramble to get them together and in the rush, forgot my daughter's bouquet.

Then when we arrived at the church, there was construction on the main street and it was shut down, so many of our guests arrived late. Since this church was hidden in a residential area, many did not know alternate routes to get there.

When we finally did start the ceremony 45-minutes late, just as we began, a construction crew began hammering construction right outside the front of the church, making it exceptionally hard for our guests to hear.

After Zoe and I exchanged our vows and sealed our union with a kiss, we headed out of the church and down the front steps. Our guests sprinkled us with rice and flower petals. We approached the limousine and climbed inside. As the limo driver focused his attention on driving, my sister cracked open a bottle of champagne. This startled the driver who had been trying to maneuver his way down a narrow one-way residential street, with cars parked on either side. Consequently, he side-swiped a car. This distracted my sister, who caused champagne to explode all over Zoe's Maid of Honor, drenching her dress, hair, and make-up. Then the driver swiped another car, then another, and then another. Only after he had finished hitting the fourth car did he finally stop the limo and step outside to assess the damage. He placed a business card on the windshield of each of these cars. He then got back in the limo and proceeded to drive us to our destination. We were on our way to have our wedding pictures taken.

Zoe's Maid of Honor pulled herself together as best she could when we arrived at the location, even using the hand dryer in a woman's public restroom to dry her dress and re-set her hair. Fortunately, the photographs went well.

Afterwards, we drove to the reception hall. When we arrived, all our guests were standing and in a state of confusion. No placecards had been set on any of the tables, so our guests did not know where to sit. Zoe immediately found the staff member responsible for this task and had photocopies of the seating arrangement made and placed on each table.

When we made our official and formal entrance, the DJ proceeded to announce our arrival by mispronouncing both of our names, introducing us backwards and incorrectly.

As we sat down to our meal, the servers presented us with the first course. Since Zoe and I had eaten a snack in the limo after the champagne incident, neither of us was hungry, so we were unable to eat. The servers quickly cleared away our barely touched food. As is customary, once the head table is cleared, all other tables are to be cleared, so we watched as the servers began taking our guests' food away, even while they were still in the middle of eating it. This continued until we asked them to slow down service, which resulted in them going into hiding for nearly half an hour, then serving dessert, then resurfacing again nearly a half hour later with coffee and tea to go with that dessert.

When dinner was finally over, the DJ proceeded to play every wrong song on the playlist. We had scratched out all the songs we did not want him to play (at the request of the DJ Company), yet those were the exact ones he played—including the *Rocky Horror Picture Show*! His mixture was so bad, if it had not been my own wedding, I would have surely walked out. Completely annoyed with the horrible music selection, I went up to the DJ and asked him to play anything from Celine

Dion. I wanted to dance with my wife and I knew Celine was one of Zoe's favorite singers. He proceeded to inconguously play "I am your Lady, you are my Man."

By the time the day was through, we were both exhausted, just as any newlyweds would be. We needed to get some sleep because at 5:30 a.m. we needed to leave for the airport to fly to Jamaica.

When we arrived at the hotel in Jamaica, they had lost our reservation for the honeymoon suite. They were so booked up, as hard as I tried, they could only provide us with a room overseeing the outdoor disco. Fatigued and left without further recourse, we retired to our room.

Upon entering, we were met by music blaring into our room so loudly, we knew it would be impossible to get some sleep. Beyond the point of frustration and exhaustion, we both tried to hold back the tears as we stepped out onto the balcony overlooking the dance floor, and watched these unknown people below us dancing, laughing and having a good time. The most devastating part for me was that their DJ was playing exactly the music selection I had hoped to receive at our own wedding.

The house, the train, and the frustrated guests.

Weeks later, after returning from our honeymoon, we went in search of our matrimonial home and found the house of our dreams. It had four bedrooms, space for an upstairs gym, an office, and a guest room for all the guests we were looking forward to inviting over. There was a hot tub outside on our back deck, and a gorgeous Roman bathroom, featuring a cream claw bath with gold taps in our master bedroom. It was more of a home than we ever expected to own. We felt so fortunate to find this house and could not believe no one had bought it before us. It was perfect for us!

We could not wait to put in our offer. It was out of our price range, but we believed that if we both worked very hard and made some extra money, we could afford it. It was a good thing we could have our own gym because our budget was so tight, we could not have possibly afforded the luxury of gym membership.

Days later, it was ours. Weeks later, when our move-in day finally arrived, we invited friends and family to help us. We planned a barbecue on our backyard deck and a dip in our outdoor hot tub for everyone. It took us only a few hours to move in. The sun was shining, the birds were chirping, and the air was fresh and clean. Having finished a hard day's work of unloading and unpacking all our personal possessions, Zoe and I, along with our friends and family, stood on the back deck, admiring all the house had to offer. Our guests were notably envious of our newfound good fortune, when all of a sudden, the first train passed by.

Conversation ceased completely. We all looked at one another in wonder and amazement as we inconspicuously tried to cover our ears from the deafening sound. For the next 60 seconds this train slowly and painstakingly blew its horn and made its way across the neighboring tracks. Zoe and I looked at each other, completely speechless.

We learned later that the trains passed day and night, week-days, weekends and even holidays. Every single time they crossed this street, the conductor would lay on the horn. It was so loud it made our dishes rattle. Although we still attempted to have guests stay overnight, they were unable to get a good night's sleep and left frustrated and exhausted.

Every attempt was unsuccessful.

Shortly after moving in, the film company I was working for underwent financial difficulty and started to cut costs. They cut down on heat in our building so much that I often needed to wear my coat while working at my computer. This continued throughout the winter.

To make matters worse, the heater in my car was not working and I could not afford to fix it. I went from freezing car to a cold day at work, only to return to the freezing car, and then drive in rush hour traffic for 1½ hours each way. I would crawl into bed cold and wake up still cold — so cold in fact, that a lukewarm shower would hurt. As this continued day after day, I believe I got a slow growing frostbite that winter. My relationship with Zoe suffered because I was the equivalent of cuddling up with an ice cube.

Finally, spring came and the bitter Canadian winter finally began to wind down. I showed up for work one sunny spring day only to find out that I had just lost my job, along with a handful of other employees, due to downsizing.

We were now in financial need. I needed a job and could not find one, so Zoe called her brother who owned a landscaping business and asked if he would consider hiring me. He hired me. So there I was, working as a landscaper, which I absolutely detested. I gained my hatred for landscaping work as a teenager, when my mother forced me to pull weeds and do gardening.

Every day I would show up for work with a painted smile on my face, take a few deep breaths, and forge through. I could not have asked for a better brother-in-law or boss. I was truly thankful for the work opportunity, but I never wanted to do that type of work to begin with, so it was a challenge for me to get up every morning.

As fall came, work slowed down and then ceased completely. I was both relieved and worried. I was relieved that I had spent months under the hot summer sun for 10-12 hours a day, doing something I despised. I was worried due to the financial predicament I was in, once again.

For the next few months, I tried to establish a small health business. I was certified in several health modalities and felt this might be a perfect time to start up a home business. All the while, Zoe was paying all the bills and expenses on her salary alone. I knew this was taking a toll on her, so after months of trying to establish my business and getting nowhere, I hesitantly and reluctantly took a job working as a manager in a fast food restaurant.

This was extremely difficult for me as I seldom ate in fast food restaurants. I often felt nauseated due to the smell of deep fried foods all over my clothes, in my hair, and on my skin.

Now our relationship suffered because I came home every night smelling like a French-fry!

Spring returned and, just as I had done for six months, I went to work at the fast food restaurant. As I was filling an order for one of the many patrons, something inside me snapped. Because of the research I had done over the years, I knew how detrimental fast food could be to the human body. I also knew how much long-term damage diet sodas caused. A parent ordered a typical child's meal, but with a diet soda and I simply could not pass that child's cup to the parent. For the first time, I felt I was personally responsible for a child's health in this fast food place, because I knew better. As a result, I had a panic attack. My heart started palpitating, and I was gasping for air. They called Zoe and she came and picked me up. I lasted another few days at that job because I could not afford to leave. Then I found another job in the newspaper that would pay me a large sum of money.

After the interview, I brought home the signed contract and showed it to Zoe. She could not help but cry out in happiness for me—that I would finally be able to match her with respect to income. But she also cried in frustration because she had worked hard all her life to rise to her salary level. Here I was, "walking in off the streets" and getting the same amount—

without a lifetime of training and hard work. Unfortunately, that job lasted only four days since I was clearly under-qualified.

Zoe was once again crushed. I sat at home for a few days until she called her brother again and asked if he would consider re-hiring me for his landscaping business. He accepted. So there I was, going back to work as a landscaper, painting that smile onto my face, and bearing yet another season.

As summer turned to fall once again, I was faced with inevitable unemployment. We tried to keep focused on each other and our relationship, but we suffered continual financial difficulties that put a great deal of strain on us. Then something happened that I did not expect.

My feelings raced; my thoughts collided.

That same fall, shortly after celebrating our second year of marriage, I came home to find Zoe soaking in a hot bubble bath in the claw bathtub of our Roman bathroom. She looked like a Greek goddess. When she looked at me with her beautiful blue eyes, I could tell that she had been crying. I bent down next to her. My hand reached out and wiped the tears from her face. "What's wrong?" I asked.

With tears pouring down her cheeks, she looked directly into my eyes. She then said something I never imagined this woman of my dreams would ever say to me. "I'm in love with another woman." She cried.

Her words ripped through my heart. My legs went out from under me. I landed on the cold ceramic floor. I was speechless.

She told me she was "Sorry," even, "So, so sorry" and that she "Never expected this to happen." Tears streamed down her face.

As she spoke, her words completely shattered my world. I had completely surrendered myself to her; to our relationship. Yet my trust and belief in her, and us, had not saved me from this devastating fate. I wanted her to go back in time, to when she first had this thought of impurity against our own sacred vows. I wanted her to choose instead to remain faithful.

I wished I had not heard this. I wished she had not said it. I wanted to hold her tighter than I had ever held her before, and I wanted to run away from her as fast as I could go—simultaneously.

I left the room to catch my breath, barely able to hear my own thoughts. My heart pounded within me. My feelings raced; my thoughts collided. I did not want to accept this reality that had been thrust upon me. With all the courage I could find within me, I did what I never imagined I would ever have to do… I walked back into the room, and with tears pouring down my face, said "I will let you go." I let her know if she wanted to be with another woman, I loved her too much to deny her true happiness. If I was not the right one for her, then I wished her well.

My ears and my heart fought against every single word I spoke. Yet with nothing left to say, I turned around and walked out. As I left the bathroom and entered our bedroom, I made my way to the edge of our bed. Without enough strength to hold myself seated, I slid off the edge of the bed and landed onto the carpeted floor below, tears clouding my vision.

I was completely and utterly crushed. I had never loved so deeply in my life. I could not even comprehend the depth of agony I experienced. I felt a death of something within me I had never felt before. I believed she was my soul mate, my other half. I trusted her with all of me: my heart, my life, my love — my future.

I sat there alone, completely vulnerable, engulfed in pain; tears drenching my cheeks. I did not know what to do — what to think, what to believe, where to go, who to turn to, who to trust, or what to do — I simply could not think clearly.

I desperately needed to understand what had just happened. I had questions I needed answers to, and answers to questions I could not figure out. My thoughts raced frantically through my head. I tried to figure out what I was supposed to do next.

I was thoroughly confused. I had loved and been hurt by a man, and I had loved and been hurt by a woman. I simply could not figure out who I was supposed to be in relationship with. I especially could not figure out God's Will or plan for my life—if there was one.

As much as I wanted to fault her, I soon realized how I had contributed to this inevitable fate. Due to all the job difficulties and financial challenges I had faced, along with the grief and guilt I felt over the loss of my children, I was frustrated, exhausted, dejected and spent. Consequently, I had little time or energy left to put into our relationship. I considered this might leave her feeling isolated and lonely. Yet, I had so many worries and concerns of my own to contend with, I had left her to sort through her own issues and concerns without my support.

It was now evidently clear my neglect had caused her pain. Now her pain rested upon me.

A few short months later, with respect and goodwill towards each other, we sold the house and went our separate ways.

Chapter Five

An Array of Wrong Results

No job, no money, no savings, no home.

I found a one-bedroom attic apartment. It was so small, there was no bedroom door; but I liked that it had a fireplace. I paid first and last month's rent, signed a lease, and moved in.

With zero money left to my name, I decided to dust myself off and restart that new business venture—a health spa. I had little business sense, even less money, but I had a good clean credit rating. (It had been seven years since the bankruptcy that followed my separation from Jake, so my credit was wiped clean.) I headed out in search of a small business loan.

I was immediately approved for $17,000 in lines of credit. I promptly spent that money securing a franchise business I was interested in pursuing. I found an unusual office space in a prime downtown location. It had a kitchenette, and a bathroom with a shower, washer and dryer. One of the health services I planned to provide was body wraps. I would need a washer and dryer. It was perfect. Before signing the lease, I was informed under no circumstance could I live there. Not planning to ever live there, I signed the one-year lease.

I needed more money, so I kept searching for funds. The more I searched, the more I was rejected. I had no idea that each application I completed for credit, whether I received it or not, lowered my credit rating. When I learned of this, I stopped; but the damage was already done. By this time, I could not even qualify for a $1,000 credit card—nor could I qualify for a cell phone lease.

With two rents now to pay, advertising costs, and living expenses, I fell further behind financially each month. I feared claiming bankruptcy for a second time. I took a part-time job on weekends to pay down my debt. Still unable to sustain my expenses; in desperation, I borrowed a large sum of money from my mother. This money allowed me to pay down my lines of credit, my car, and all overdue expenses. I also loaned $5,000 to a business associate who had also been struggling. For a moment I felt financially relieved.

That relief lasted only two months. My overall monthly expenses were too much. I could no longer afford both my apartment rent, and office rent. To avoid borrowing from my already paid down lines of credit, I paid the penalty to break the apartment lease and moved out. I clandestinely moved into my office. I cooked on a hot plate, and slept on the floor. At night I stressed at the thought of getting caught living there. During the day I tried desperately to grow my business and stay positive, but without money to advertise, I could not bring in new clients; without clients, I received no income. Each month my expenses came due. I sank deeper and deeper into debt with no apparent way out.

Ten months after Zoe and I had separated, I was in debt for $75,000. I had no job, no money, no savings, no home, and nothing to show for it—I was financially worse than broke. I needed to close down my business. With nowhere left to go, I contemplated living in my car.

"Bad Luck"

Since our separation, I had become close to Zoe's sister— my ex sister-in-law, Sarah. We were very close in age and we both had motherhood in common. We quickly became best friends. She inevitably learned of the full extent of my financial woes.

That was when Sarah came to my office one day to let me know that she had spoken with her husband, Mark, and they had agreed that I could have their guest room in the basement until my life got back on track. Shocked, but grateful, I reluctantly agreed. I was shocked because I never expected such a gracious offer. I was reluctant because I did not want to impose. I was grateful because I truly had no other place to go.

They had both known me for a few years already, since they attended my wedding to Zoe. They had general knowledge of everything I had experienced in my life since they had come to be a part of it.

In February 2004, I moved into the basement bedroom of their suburban home, 1½ hours from Toronto. It was warm, quaint, and I felt very comfortable there. I knew I needed to find a job but it was a challenge. As I searched through the newspaper, I spotted an ad for a blackjack dealer in a casino. I knew nothing about dealing but it claimed to offer training and a "guaranteed position," so I decided to do it. The training was in Toronto, so I would have to commute back and forth.

I called to register and the following week I began training. It was expensive. I would have to use my line of credit to pay for it, but thought it would be worth it since a job was guaranteed. In lieu of room and board, I agreed to help Sarah deliver newspapers in the middle of the night.

Soon I found myself up at 1:30 every morning, in the bitter cold, delivering newspapers until breakfast. Then I would head into Toronto for training which required me to multiply numbers in my head all day long. I would return home to eat, sleep for a couple hours, then wake up and do it all over again.

This went on for several weeks. I became so exhausted that I was not paying attention to the ice on the driveway, and I slipped and fell. Instinctively, I tried to break my fall with my left arm. Before the night was through, I slipped again, bracing myself once again with my left arm, only this time, my entire arm throbbed from wrist to shoulder.

I struggled to continue training, knowing I needed to because it would guarantee me a job. I found it excruciatingly painful since the dealing of the cards required me to use my left arm in repetitive motion.

Two months later, in April, I finally completed my training, was qualified, and went for the job interview. I was excited to start the job because, at that point, I had not worked for a while and was desperate for money. I got the job, but they told me I would not start for another two months.

By the time June arrived, I was finally able to start; I thought my luck would turn around once I got the job. The first three months, I was able to pay down some of my debt, but then my luck changed once again. I stepped off a dark staircase and tore ligaments in my foot. I had to walk with crutches, which further aggravated my already injured shoulder. The casino suspended me from work because of my injury. My finances fell deeper into arrears after I was denied government financial assistance through Employment Insurance benefits. I was a mere 23-hours short, so I did not qualify. Soon my lines of credit once again became maxed out. I could no longer afford my health supplements, consequently my health diminished to the point that I became allergic to practically everything. I was continuously ill and could not recover.

As Christmas neared, I became depressed because I knew I could not afford to buy gifts for my children. I sought professional help for this depression but refused to take the medication, because I had never taken prescription medication before and the thought of taking it made me even more depressed. So instead, I simply suffered through the depression.

When my foot finally healed I looked forward to returning to work, but the crutches I had been using had reinjured my shoulder so badly it was preventing me from working properly. I had to resign from my casino job, and once again, had no job.

I was in a state of financial ruin once again. It became clear that I was in no financial position to leave my host's home anytime soon. I had no options I could think of for getting out of the mess I was in.

Since I had arrived on Sarah's doorstep twelve months earlier, she and her husband had witnessed one event after another that kept me from progressing forward in my life. It left them both shaking their heads in awe and disbelief. They marveled at how anyone could possibly go through so much "bad luck"—for lack of a better term.

Sarah never faltered.

Unintentionally, I let Sarah know I had loaned a business acquaintance $5,000 because her business was faltering, like mine had been. This acquaintance agreed to sign a promissory note to repay the money within three months. Although I had tried reaching her several times over the months that followed, she was clearly trying to avoid me. I had gotten to the place where I thought the money was lost for good, when Sarah let me know that she would help me get the money back. I was optimistic but also reserved. I did not dare get my hopes up because I believed if I did not expect anything good to happen, I would not be disappointed when it didn't.

Sarah remained hopeful however, and let me know that nobody is supposed to owe anybody any debt. With that, she said a quick prayer for me to get back what was rightfully mine. As she prayed, I somehow felt disconnected, like she was hopeful, but I was just standing there next to her. Her request did not seem to be getting granted. Numerous times, we attempted to contact the woman who owed me the money, but she had moved. Though I nearly lost hope many times, Sarah never did. Due to her refusal to give up, she did eventually find out where the woman lived. I was both shocked and grateful.

It became clear that our next step would be to go to court to recover this $5,000. As I prepared for the court date, I could not find the promissory note I had written up. I feared I had purged it when I closed down my business. Feeling less than prepared to defend my case, once again I began to feel hopeless. Sarah never faltered. She stood steadfast in her conviction that no one was to owe anyone money and that I deserved to be paid back. This brought some hope back.

We both realized that it was more than the money we were going after. The money now represented a new beginning for me. It would allow me to find a new home and enable me to pay down first and last month's rent. I would also be able to repay $2,000 of what I currently owed Sarah and Mark. They had loaned me that money when I was unable to work.

The scheduled court date finally arrived. With Sarah's guidance and support, I walked into court to face my former business associate. She never showed up. When the judge asked for evidence of the $5,000 loan, I presented him with a copy of the cancelled cheque, on which I had written in the memo "loan." That was all he needed to rule that she owed me the money. With that, he granted me authority to receive the funds. I asked him when I could expect to receive the money. He told me he had no way of knowing—it was up to me to go after it. All he could do was determine that she owed me the money, the rest was up to me. I went to the court clerks and they reviewed all the documentation I could present. They too let me know there was nothing more they could do for me. I was shocked. I had always assumed once a judge would make such a ruling, that the money would somehow automatically be given as well.

What had started out to be promising had quickly turned into disappointment. With my day in court now over, I returned home exhausted and puzzled. Even at this point, Sarah never gave up hope. Unlike her, I had grown accustomed to a life of failure and disappointment. When I looked at her, she was empathic towards me but I also recognized that she had a genuine hopefulness that one day soon, all this would work out and I would receive that money. I could not understand how she remained so optimistic, but I was thankful for her unwillingness to give up. I knew she had the strength and hope that I needed when I simply could not find it for myself.

While all this had been going on, whenever I was able to escape the little town that I now lived in (that had no homosexuals anywhere in sight), I would go downtown to the gay part of town. I was not looking for a new life partner, I just wanted to find refuge and feel connected to all that seemed normal and familiar to me.

Hellish merry-go-round.

I did not realize the extent of my problems until my life was measured against Sarah and Mark's family of five, who altogether, had not faced as much adversity as I alone had within the single year I lived there. Only then did all the unjust events in my life finally come to light. I was astounded to witness a family of five go through their lives so effortlessly while my life was going awry at each new unplanned and unexpected turn. Comparatively, the unexpected incidences that did come up in their lives would somehow get resolved and dissipate without incident or concern. They just seemed to know what to do and how to handle every situation, even those they had never been through before. Their home was a place of refuge, serenity and peace. Above all, they had a lot of fun together; lots of laughter, no cause for stress, and no worries.

Other than Mark and Sarah, I did not associate with any other Christian family. I thought living that way (outside of church on Sundays) would be boring and empty of good times and fun; but their lives were far from boring and they were certainly not missing out on fun. In fact, they were having a blast. I was the one missing out.

I felt like I had been living my life on a hellish merry-go-round that would only stop to let me off in a deeper pit than the one I had just crawled out of. I desperately wanted off…

Chapter Six

Asking Questions to Receive Insight

"May I ask you a few questions?"

It was a cold wintery evening in March 2005 when I had finally come to the realization that something had to change to stop the insanity my life had become. I needed normalcy and I knew I could not find it on my own. I had tried, but the more I tried, the worse things got.

I recognized the great opportunity that I had immediately in front of me. Here was a family that I was privileged to live with and observe. They had what I wanted. I realized if I wanted what they had, I needed to understand what they knew.

After dinner that evening, I noticed Mark sitting in his favorite chair in the corner of the living room, drinking a hot cup of coffee. He was quietly reading an old familiar book that

I had often seen him read before, so I decided to make myself a hot cup of tea and join him. I nestled comfortably into the loveseat that was directly opposite him, wrapped a blanket around my legs and took a sip of tea. He looked up at me as I sat down and gave me his usual grin through the burly beard that encased his upper lip and chin. (If not for the dimples that folded the beard on his cheeks his smile would have been hard to identify, though the gentleness in his eyes could seem to smile all on their own.) At 6'2" and robust in stature, he was somehow not intimidating. Sarah would often refer to him as her great big teddy bear.

As I sat there, I noticed the pile of books that seemed permanently placed next to him on the side table. All these books were big, like textbooks and most were larger than the one he was reading and currently held on his lap. As I sat there quietly observing him, I wondered what he could possibly be looking up in that book and what information he could possibly hope to find in there.

Just then, Sarah sat down on the sofa facing both Mark and me, forming a triangle so we could all comfortably see one another. She too gathered a comforter from the back of the sofa and pulled it over her lap. She fluffed up the pillow next to her, reached over for her cup of tea, and then glanced at me with a quiet smile as she took a sip.

We all sat there in quiet comfort. Five years prior, I had not even known this family, yet here I was a part of it now, feeling welcomed, invited and like I belonged. I had found myself in a desperate situation a year prior and this was the family that opened up their home to me; not just their physical house, but their home, inviting me to become a part of their family.

Who were these Christians who had shown me so much generosity and compassion, made me feel at peace, and lived in peace themselves? Why was I able to simply sit in their presence and feel serenity, calmness, and not have a care in the world? What was it that they had in their lives that I did not? I had been exposed to the exact same surroundings, the same environment, and the same circumstances for an entire year, yet my life kept getting messed up and theirs was not. I both wanted and needed to know.

"Mark?" I quietly interrupted, "may I ask you a few questions?"

He closed the book on his lap, and focused his attention upon me. "Sure, what would you like to know?"

The thought of everything that I had gone through and experienced since I had moved in came to mind and I knew they had been witness to it all.

"With everything that's gone wrong over the past year since I've lived here, I've noticed that you and your family haven't gone through the same sorts of struggles and difficulties as I have," I began. He nodded. "I was just wondering, do most people go through this much difficulty in their lives?"

Both he and Sarah shook their heads no, in sync. He let me know that it was not at all typical and that he had never seen anyone else go through this much difficulty in such a short time.

"Why do you suppose my life has been such a mess and yours has remained so peaceful?" I wanted to know.

"Possibly because we choose to live our lives the right way instead of our own way; we don't follow our feelings or let them dictate our choices; and we ensure we're not breaking any divine laws or principles along the way," Mark answered thoughtfully.

"But I thought I had the free will to live my life however I choose to?"

"You do."

"Then how come my life managed to get messed up if I was simply exercising my own free will?" If this was the case, it did not seem very free to me.

"For the same reason we cannot drink water or vodka in equal measure—one will destroy our life, the other will save it."

He had a point.

"So how's it working for you so far?"

"Now may I ask *you* a few questions?" he asked while taking a sip of coffee.

I nodded.

"You've been living your life your way until now, thinking, believing, and doing what you believe to be right, and living your life the best way you know how; am I right?"

I nodded again.

"So how's it working for you so far?" he asked me.

"How's what working?"

"How's it all working for you? How's your life in general? Are the choices and decisions you've made for yourself, and continue to make for yourself working in your life? How's your job situation? Your financial situation? Your family situation? Are you happy, successful and healthy? Do you sleep well at night? Is your reality lining up with your dreams? Do you have lots of moments of peace, happiness and joy…or is it something else?"

"It's definitely something else," I admitted.

"Is that how you choose to live out the rest of your life?" he asked.

I shook my head no. I knew without a doubt that I did not want to continue to live out the rest of my life in the mess that it had become. I wanted the type of life that I had witnessed his family living. I wanted the peace and happiness—not all the turmoil.

I shared my thoughts with Mark, letting him know my life had not turned out at all the way I had hoped or dreamed it would. I told him that ever since my common-law husband assaulted me, and then I discovered I was gay, I had been travelling a very difficult path (to say the least). I felt the struggle to get society to approve of me so that I could feel comfortable and be outwardly open and gay, without fear of being judged. I was also frustrated that no matter how hard I tried to make things work out, they would not work out the way I hoped or planned. I had tried to move out of their house for a year already and every time something would happen financially that prevented me. I felt stuck because I could not seem to move out or move forward in my life. To me it seemed evident that I was just plagued with "bad luck" and their family was fortunate to have "good luck."

"Do you really believe you have bad luck?" he asked.

It certainly appeared that way to me.

"What if I told you it has nothing to do with luck, and if you want what you refer to as 'good luck,' you can have it for yourself."

I was intrigued yet hesitant.

"Many people who appear to have 'good luck' in life are in reality just following divine law. Similarly, those who appear to have 'bad luck' are often going against divine law—knowingly or unknowingly," he explained.

I still was not sure what the right way was. I had only ever followed my feelings my whole life, and I had never even heard of divine laws before. I needed to understand how all this translated into how greatly my life differed from theirs. He stated so many things I did not understand; it made me curious to learn more.

"Are these laws and principles you're referring to associated with any sort of religion?" I asked.

"No," he answered. "They are in the unseen realm, but they are as real and tangible as love, air and gravity. We are all governed by these laws which, without exception, affect everyone equally, regardless of race, ethnicity, age, color, gender, lifestyle preference, sexual orientation, social status, or religious beliefs."

He was giving me a lot to think about.

What exactly is free will for?

I needed greater clarification about free will.

"According to the way you understand free will, what would be the ultimate intention or purpose of having it in the first place?" Mark asked me. "How much of this free will do you believe you actually have? Are there any restrictions on free will? If there are restrictions, then how could it be considered 'free will' in the freest sense of the word?"

I did not have any answers. I was still processing all he said when he continued with a barrage of questions.

"If each and every one of us has been given this free will in order to live our lives here on earth the way we personally choose to live it, then wouldn't there also be some provision included so that we would not be stopped or hindered by laws, or be in conflict with the free will of other people? Wouldn't there be a simple, straightforward way to ensure that everybody, everywhere, all at the same time, would be able to follow their own free will and still have the world run smoothly? After all, if this was really the full intention of free will, then why should any one of us expect anything less than a perfect world run by everybody's personal free will, all acting out at any time, any place, anywhere?

"Shouldn't we expect that it would come to us without any repercussions? After all, if there are repercussions, wouldn't that negate the very concept and premise of free will? Shouldn't this free will that we have allow us to do anything we want to do, for example; to rob a bank, jump off a tall building, or even to kill someone? If we do in fact have free will to live our lives any way that *we choose*, then shouldn't we be able to expect that free will to have no conditions? Shouldn't our free will supersede any restrictions, even of laws?"

What he said made me think, but I had no answers to his questions. "So what do you believe our free will is for?" I asked.

"Not to do whatever we want, whenever we want, but to make the right choice rather than the wrong one." Then he looked at me, smiled and said, "Now you have the free will to believe what I say, or not."

I hesitated. Why would he say I had the free will to believe him or not? I thought to myself *he would not make much of a sales guy—making that kind of statement after such a pitch.* Then it dawned on me... this was not a pitch. It was the very essence of what free will was all about.

Laws, curses and blessings.

I knew I needed to comprehend more about these laws, so I asked Mark to explain them to me.

"There are three types of laws." He expounded. There are *Societal laws* which are manmade and can be amended or changed to suit society's needs. There are *Natural laws,* such as the law of gravity, which cannot be changed, the breaking of which often leads to physical harm or injury regardless of ignorance, disbelief or denial. Finally, there are *Divine laws,* which exist in the unseen spiritual realm, and are as consistent and unchangeable as natural laws. When we obey and follow these laws and principles, our life is good and blessed; when we break them, our life cannot be blessed, consequently it becomes what's referred to as cursed.

Mark let me know many people struggle trying to chase after what they want in life: an abundance of money, nice clothes, nice car, big house, the latest in electronics, a good job, but what they do not realize is that all these are a result of having our life blessed. If we are not living our life the right way it cannot be blessed so it becomes cursed; which results in us experiencing difficulties receiving or keeping such things. Furthermore, our job, finances, health, relationships, and mental and emotional well-being also become affected.

I had never heard of life being blessed or cursed before.

"What is it like to live a cursed life?" I was curious to know.

"*Mentally*, we are confused," Mark began. "We don't know what to do, and we don't know where to find the solutions or answers. The pressures of life can tempt us to turn to vices to help us cope. We live in fear of a variety of things, including failure and the unknown." *Emotionally,* we are stressed. We are hurt and feel misunderstood, mistreated, not accepted and even rejected. We are angry, frustrated or anxious. We try to fix our problems ourselves or by seeking advice from others, but more often than not, we find ourselves in another mess — sometimes in an even greater mess. *Relationally* — we are broken. In spite of our best attempts, we find ourselves in failed marriages and relationships. Our families are torn apart with separations and divorces, and any children we may have suffer the consequences, having to leave one parent to spend time with the other. This results in us unwittingly carrying baggage into future relationships. *Financially,* we are in debt. We work more to get ahead, but no matter how hard we work, we cannot seem to get ahead. *Physically,* we are exhausted due to our busy schedule. We become tired and worn out. Our health suffers from overwork and lack of rest.

My life fit Mark's description of a cursed life almost exactly. I was stressed, frustrated and confused. I was deeply in debt, my family and relationships were broken, I was exhausted and unhealthy, I struggled to chase after what I wanted, and felt I would never get ahead.

I was anxious to find out what it would be like to live a blessed life.

"To be blessed means we have an empowerment to succeed in everything we do," Mark said. *Mentally,* we have a sound mind and clear thinking. We have the ability to make proper decisions and know where to find the answers to any problem or challenge we may face. Then we can face these challenges peacefully and without worry or stress. *Emotionally,* we are stable in our thoughts, feelings and emotions, and have control over them instead of being subjected to them. *Relationally,* we have good solid relationships with friends and family based on love and respect. *Financially,* we are debt-free and even have an abundance of money—more than enough to provide for all our financial needs, and to help others in need. *Physically,* we are strong, healthy and healed of all sickness and disease. We have sound, restful sleep and wake up refreshed and ready to face the day.

I was shocked to learn about divine laws and principles along with the resulting blessings and curses because I had no idea they even existed. Yet there was a clear difference between following divine law and living a life that is blessed, versus not following divine law and living a life that is cursed.

"How is it possible that I have never heard of divine laws, principles, blessings and curses before?" I asked.

"You were simply never taught," Mark answered.

He knew that I had been raised to live a healthy lifestyle, so he used that as an example. That it was normal for me and I knew it worked. But to those who were not aware and who had not experienced it for themselves, a healthy lifestyle would seem strange and unusual. The same holds true for understanding divine laws and principles (which he referred to as living a spiritual lifestyle, since it operates in the unseen spiritual realm). People not raised to live a spiritual lifestyle could find it strange and unusual, while those who knew and experienced it, knew its benefits and how well it worked.

"What do I need to do to stop my life from being cursed?" I asked.

"Make different lifestyle choices," he said.

An alcoholic, a liar, an adulterer and a Nanny.

I wanted to know how making different choices could stop my life from being cursed.

He went on to explain that drinking alcohol is not a wrong lifestyle choice, but becoming a drunkard or alcoholic is. Yet for an alcoholic, drinking alcohol is not the problem, after all, it is socially acceptable. One can buy alcohol in restaurants, bars, clubs, sporting events and in stores. There is even a designated age when people are legally allowed to consume it. As such, alcohol is often viewed as a rite of passage into adulthood. To an alcoholic, drinking is what makes sense. In fact, many alcoholics do not have a problem with drinking, they have a problem being sober. Oftentimes, what started out as drinking to make them feel better, turns into something that makes them feel bad if they are not doing it.

To a liar, lying is acceptable, yet lying is a wrong lifestyle choice. Society frequently tries to make allowances for 'little white lies,' but the reality is, all lies are wrong. Little white lies are often told to protect the liar's freedom to begin with. Once they get away with the lie, the very nature of lies forces them to have to tell another lie to cover up the first one. Soon the lies become bigger and more intertwined with one another. Eventually the liar's entire life turns into one huge web of lies. Inevitably, the liar can no longer tell the lies from the truth and his or her life can end up being ruled by their lies. The freedom they tried to protect in the beginning is the same freedom they completely lose control over in the end.

To an adulterer, adultery appears to solve their problem, not create one. It is emotionally driven and offers love, acceptance and approval, often deemed to be lacking in the marriage to begin with. The adulterer's marriage and family remains intact, so no one seems to be getting hurt. (Besides, in movies, television shows and sitcoms, adultery is often-times portrayed as normal.) However, the very thing the adulterer was seeking to gain and keep in the beginning is the very thing they wind up losing in the end. They lose love, acceptance and the approval of friends and family once they are found out. Often, they lose everything else associated with that marriage: children, relatives, home, finances, and often, even the person with whom they had the adulterous affair.

He explained that although each of these experiences appear to differ from one another as we would view them, they are all in fact very much the same: they all oppose divine law. As a result, the person's life cannot be blessed. They lose peace, happiness and hope. In some cases, they lose health and finances as well.

What started out as a personal free will choice, winds up taking control over their life, consuming every aspect of it until they inevitably lose the very freedom they once had to make that free will choice to begin with.

Mark suggested the movie *Nanny McPhee* as a great illustration of how our own personal choices affect our lives.

Nanny McPhee is a movie about a governess who tames the wild natures of seven children. They desire to do whatever they want to do and refuse to do as they are told. She carries a walking stick, and whenever she asks the children to stop their wrong behavior and they refuse to, she taps her walking stick onto the floor and immediately they are released into their very own desires. They find that the desires they fought to keep end up holding them captive, and discover their own behavior is completely out of their control, resulting in a mess.

She watches over them as their very own desires bring some of them to tears. Soon, they start begging her to stop their out of control behavior. At which time, she agrees to do so only after they express a willingness to do the right thing instead. As soon as they submit to her request, she releases them from the bondages of their desires and their out of control behavior stops immediately. She then also cleans up the mess they made.

"This is a lot like how God works in our lives," Mark explained. When we insist on doing something our way—even to the point where our desires become totally out of our control—He will not impede on our free will choice to do whatever we want, even when it is causing us pain. That is, until and unless we ask Him to make it stop. However, He can only make it stop if we are willing to do the right thing instead. When we are willing to do this, He will stop our out of control behavior and clean up the mess we have made.

Chapter Seven

Viewing Life a Whole New Way

"No."

What Mark said was opening up my eyes, ears and mind to a whole new way of viewing life. It was becoming clear that unless I decided to make a change in my life, the now identifiable curses and struggles I had been facing would continue.

Although I was tempted to hold onto the thought that only desperate and destitute people were in some sort of relationship with God, I realized that Mark and Sarah claimed to be and neither of them (nor any of their three children) was desperate or destitute like I was! Try as I might, I could not refute the facts; I was the one whose life was messed up, not theirs.

I decided to ask Mark the burning question that I desperately needed answered. The gay preacher promised that God loves and accepts homosexuals. I needed to verify this as truth.

"Does the God you believe in accept homosexuals?" I asked.

He looked over at Sarah and she looked back at him. Then he fixed his eyes on me, nodded his head and said, "Yes."

I sighed in relief, assured that I was living my life perfectly and in line with His plan for me. I began to feel confident that I was on the correct path, when suddenly my self-righteous thoughts were interrupted. After all, we had been discussing the mess my life had become. I looked back at Mark questioningly, and without saying a word, he declared, "But He also loves and accepts thieves, lairs, and adulterers."

Now I was confused. I did not know much about the Bible, but I knew one thing for sure—the Ten Commandments. I knew three of the ten stated that we are not supposed to steal, lie, or commit adultery. So why had Mark just said what he did? I looked at him in complete confusion, but he just sat quietly and patiently, not saying a word. He was waiting for me. In the silence, I realized what Mark was waiting for: for me to recognize that I had not asked the appropriate question.

In my mind, I pondered what Mark had just told me. God accepted the thief, but stealing is not acceptable? He accepted the liar, but lying is not acceptable? He accepted the adulterer, but committing adultery is not acceptable?

It was clear that He accepted the person but not the behavior. Upon this realization, I dared to ask him the more appropriate question to get the answer I was truly seeking: "Does God accept homosexuality and homosexual behavior?" That is when the answer came that I dreaded. His answer was short, brief, and absolutely unwavering.

"No."

Upon hearing this, my feelings and thoughts began to race — at war with one another. I had been led to believe that if God accepted homosexuals, He also accepted homosexuality.

At first, I did not want to believe Mark. I wanted to defend myself. I hoped he was wrong or mistaken. I wished the answer would have been anything other than what he said — a simple, firm, unquestionable, irrefutable, undeniable, irrevocable, "No."

Exhausted in my own mind and in my own thoughts, I sat completely numb, staring blankly. "No" resonated in my ears and echoed in my mind. Such a simple word, yet the truth that stood behind that single word had the ultimate power to change my entire life. I was faced with an existential moment of choice — would I choose to believe Mark or not?

Questions flooded my mind. What about my feelings of being gay? What about the possibility that I was born like this? What about legislation being passed that affirmed same-sex rights? I needed answers and clarification, desperately.

I'll prove you wrong.

After taking a minute to think and leaning to the possibility that he was wrong, other thoughts entered my mind. A flood of memories rushed in: of dreams gone awry, plans and goals buried and vanished, and flashes of a life I had lived full of difficulty, pain, frustration and more. All this surfaced and brought me back to the reality of what led me to ask Mark the question in the first place.

I had always assumed that if I were truly living my life incorrectly, I would have been given me some sort of a sign to let me know I was headed down the wrong path. I asked Mark if I this was true.

"Figuratively speaking," he said, "if we're heading in the wrong direction, doors will be shut that will make it very difficult for us to continue in it."

Just then, I remembered the door to the women's nightclub being closed to me when I tried to go there the third time. When I shared this with Mark, he nodded, smiled and told me, "That's very much in line with how things happen in our lives—not that there are always physical doors that shut like the one you experienced, but doors of opportunity will be closed."

He explained that closed doors often present themselves as resistance, frustration, anxiety, hurt, pain, and the feeling of mistreatment or being misunderstood. Constantly trying to prove ourselves, or battling to move forward are often indicators that we are heading in the wrong direction. These are stop signs. We can plow forward and keep moving forward through them, that is our free will choice, but if we do we will likely miss out on the good life we were supposed to have.

Likewise, when we are walking the right way, doors to good opportunities will open for us that we may not have been able to open for ourselves. These opportunities often come to us effortlessly and wind up enriching our life with success and promotion.

"So what can I expect to happen in my life if I simply stopped being gay?" I wanted to know.

"Everything that's broken in your life would be fixed, and everything you've lost will be restored." He stated.

I pondered this for a moment...

"So you're telling me, if I simply chose to stop living a non-straight lifestyle, my whole life would completely turn around; I would gain back *everything* I've lost, and have everything fixed that's been broken?" I questioned explicitly, believing this suggestion to be so farfetched that it could not possibly be true.

"Yes," he stated.

He said this with such an air of confidence; the only thing that came to my mind was *"there's no way... that's not even possible... I'll prove you wrong."* Then I heard a voice in my head say, *"he's telling the truth."*

Gay, out, and proud—not straight.

Mark shared with me that there is a divine principle that states we will become whatever we call ourselves. He asked what I had been saying about my own life and whether or not I had ever called myself gay, out, and proud—not straight. I agreed I had. He then asked if I had ever taken the time to find out what those words truly meant. I shook my head "no."

"Can you define what you think these words mean?" Mark asked.

I responded with these definitions: **gay** (not straight)**, out** (other people knowing about it)**, proud** (happy to be gay), and **straight** (not gay).

He nodded in acknowledgment, then handed me a dictionary and asked me to look up the actual meanings for each of these words.

First, I looked up "pride" because I had attended Gay Pride parades: *the state or quality of being proud*. I looked up the word "proud": *a high or inordinate opinion of one's own dignity, importance, merit, or superiority, conceit, arrogance*.

"I'm not sure I understand," I said. I always thought pride and being proud was a good thing. It did not appear to be true. I asked him to clarify.

"Pride can be either a good thing or a bad thing, depending on the circumstance and situation," Mark explained. "It's a good thing when a parent is proud of a child because their child makes a good or proper decision. We can also be proud of ourselves when we abstain from doing the wrong thing, especially when we're tempted."

"The pride that would be wrong is the kind where we believe and trust only in our own thoughts and opinions. This leaves little room for correction or redirection of misguided beliefs. When we do anything our way instead of God's way, we are being prideful. God actually abhors the proud."

I was shocked.

I looked up the next word, "out": *obliterate, undecipher-able, not open to consideration… senseless… to be deprived… Not in power, authority, or the like… In a state of disagreement; quarrelling; at odds… Unsuitable to the circumstances or surroundings."*

"Wow," was all I could say. I had just read for myself that being "out" meant many things I had not expected nor intended to call myself.

I then looked up the word, "gay": *Licentious (unrestrained by law or general morality; immoral)."* The definition continued: *Gay has had senses dealing with sexual conduct since the 17th century. A gay woman was a prostitute, a gay man a womanizer, a gay house a brothel. Gay as an adjective meaning "homosexual" goes back at least to the 1930s. After World War II, as social attitudes toward sexuality began to change, gay was applied openly by homosexuals to themselves…".*

I shook my head, trying to understand why homosexuals would choose this word to describe themselves when the original meaning was far different than how it was used today. According to this definition, a man who called himself gay back in the 17th century was admitting that he was a womanizer. Likewise a self-professed gay woman would be calling herself a prostitute; so whether a womanizer or a prostitute, a gay person was generally disrespectful of members of the opposite sex. The word "gay" did not arise as a term for genuine love between two same-sex people, but was a term of disrespect toward a member of the opposite sex.

I was flabbergasted to learn the true meanings of these three words I had so proudly used to label myself. The stunned look on my face prompted Mark to tell me to look up the word "straight."

The definition of "straight" read: *Direct in character, candid, honest, honorable, upright, reliable, factual, objective, cogent, rational, being in the proper order or condition, continuous, unbroken, thoroughgoing, complete, virtuous… in possession of truth or facts… without embellishment."*

I was absolutely astounded.

"So, whenever anyone claims to be not-straight, then they are in fact stating they are none of what you last read, regardless of what they may believe they are saying," he stated. "Is that what you intended to call yourself when you claimed to be 'gay, out, and proud—not straight'?" he asked me.

I shook my head.

"Since you have the dictionary open, look up the word 'sin,'" he suggested.

So I did. The definition for "sin" read: *against divine law.*

Had I been duped?

When I initially asked Mark about homosexuality, I did desperately want to know the truth, and when I finally heard the
truth, I was relieved. But that relief lasted for only a moment,
because before I could go on in my own thoughts, the rest of the
truth came crashing down on me like a ton of bricks.

I was shocked because, enclosed within this truth, I also came
to the full realization that if *God does not accept homosexual
behavior*, then that means *He could not have possibly created
me as a homosexual*. This led me to the realization that if He had
not created me as one, then I must have created myself to be one,
through my own thoughts of what I believed to be true and real,
influenced by others who shared the same thoughts. This being
the case, if I was the one who created myself as a homosexual,
then the life I had been living for the past thirteen years was fal-
sified by my own misguided thoughts, imagination and beliefs.

Homosexuality had become my way of life. It was all encom-
passing and controlled my way of thinking, my way of believing,
what I did, what I felt, and how I behaved. It determined the
places I would go and the people I would hang out with. It was
what defined who I was and who I would become. It was all of
me. I could not even imagine what I would need to do to stop,

nor did I know where to start. All I knew was that after thirteen years, I had to start somewhere.

"Is there the remotest possibility that I was born this way?" I asked one final time.

"Absolutely," he said. "We were all born with various tendencies, wanting to live our life our own way, but that doesn't mean we're supposed to live like that. An alcoholic may have been born with a tendency to drink alcohol due to an alcoholic parent, but he may also have learned the behavior by imitating others or due to their influence. Still, that person was not created by God to become or remain an alcoholic. If he insists on continuing to drink and on remaining an alcoholic, he will eventually end up losing out and missing out on many good things he could have had, including a good life. If we insist on living our life our way, following our own tendencies, we too will miss out on the good life we were supposed to have."

The price I had to pay to learn the truth about homosexuality had already cost me everything. I had lost my children, my spouse, my home, my job, my savings, my health, my peace, and my hope.

I never intended to live my life the wrong way or to suffer the consequences of making wrong lifestyle choices. That is why I walked into a church all those years ago to begin with. I desperately wanted to know the truth and I wanted to receive assurance that I was making the right decision for my life.

"How could I have been so misled?" I wanted to know.

"You've been duped," was all he said.

"Had I been duped?" I wondered. When I looked up the word "duped" in the dictionary, I was surprised to learn that I actually had been duped: *A person who is easily deceived or fooled. A person who unquestioningly or unwittingly serves a cause or another person. To make a dupe of; deceive; delude; trick.* This acronym and further insights from the dictionary pressed the point even more:

D – Deluded: to mislead the mind or judgment.

U – Unquestioning: not open to doubt or question.

P – Person: a human being; a man, woman, or child.

E – Easily: with ease; without trouble; beyond question.

D – Deceived: to mislead by a false appearance or statement; trick.

So there I was, a <u>deluded</u>, <u>unquestioning</u> <u>person</u>, who had been <u>easily</u> <u>deceived</u> (aka tricked!).

Last Will and Testament.

"Do you want to know what God's Will is for your life?" Mark asked me. I absolutely wanted to know. I wondered for years, but still had not figured it out.

"It is God's Will that we inherit the Kingdom of God," he told me.

What he said triggered a memory of what the priest in the Catholic Church had told me all those years ago: If I lived a homosexual lifestyle not that I would go to hell, but rather I would not inherit this Kingdom. I needed to know what this meant, so I asked him.

"Most people believe God's Will means what He expects *from* us, and it does, but it also means what He wants to *get* to us," Mark explained.

I had never heard of this before and was curious to learn more.

He explained that just like a man who leaves his "Last Will and Testament," dispersing an inheritance to his loved ones after he dies, the Bible was left for us with a similar purpose in that the contents of which is actually His Will and Testament to us. It actually talks about things we are supposed to "inherit" from

Him and is filled with things He wants to provide for us, do for us, and get to us.

It also offers truth, guidance and direction to help us make good and right decisions for all areas of our life including: our finances, health, and relationships.

"Is that what God's Will truly means?" I asked.

"Yes," he replied. "It is His Will for us to inherit all of His blessings so we can have a good life and take pleasure in all things: have fun, be with our family, laugh, have peace, joy, a great job, no financial worries, and be in good health. There is so much He wants to get to us, all we need to do is let Him. Then we can look forward to inheriting all of this."

"How do you know all this is true?" I wanted to know.

"Because it works." he simply stated.

I was astounded.

"What could I expect to inherit for my life now, since I've lost so much?" I questioned.

"You can expect to inherit every good thing in your life that would make it happy, peaceful and complete. You can expect to have your health regained, a stable job, your finances in order, and be debt-free. You can also expect the relationship with your children and family restored." He said, "When you live your life right, '*All these blessings will come upon you.*'" [1]

Everything he said to me was more than I could ever hope to receive. I had lost so much for so long, it was hard to believe that I could possibly receive any of those things back.

"We're here to experience life in abundance—to the full, until it overflows. Our Creator is good and loving, is not boring, and didn't create us to be boring. He is unique, fun, adventurous and exciting—He created us to be the same," Mark said.

I had never heard life expressed like this before. It sounded amazing.

Too accurate and detailed to be coincidental.

I asked Mark if he could show me any examples from my own life that he might be aware of, where I had been experiencing curses. I wanted to see how it would manifest itself in my life.

Mark rose to the challenge and helped me to understand what curses had come into my life. He proceeded to present this information to me the way that I needed him to—straightforward, direct, and with evidence to support his claims.

He recalled the legal battles I endured for six years trying to maintain custody of my children. The many sleepless nights filled with tears, worry, dread and confusion; and how I wished each night that it was day because I could not sleep, and how I wished each day that it was night because I was so exhausted. He let me know the curse reads: *"You will live in constant suspense, filled with dread both night and day, never sure of your life. In the morning you will say, 'If only it were evening!' and in the evening, 'If only it were morning!'"* [2]

I had lost my children to their father who worked hard to take them away from me. The curse reads: *"You will have sons and daughters but you will not keep them because they will go into captivity."* [3]

As for my many jobs and everything I did to get ahead; no matter how hard I tried, something would always happen to put me back behind. The curse reads: *"...you will be unsuccessful in everything you do..."* [4]

In regard to Zoe and me finding our dream home, and recognizing that paying for it stole from us our solitude and the comfort a home was supposed to bring. The curse reads: *". . . the house which your hands have made will never be your resting-place."* [5]

As for as my health, and how I had always valued good health and feared having any sort of sickness or disease come upon me—yet had experienced ill health to the point where I was continuously ill and could not seem to recover. The curse reads: *"…all the diseases…of which you were afraid…they will cling to you."* [6]

Mark also let me know that some of the curses that came into my life were because I accepted a homosexual lifestyle, but some of them also appeared because I was in only a common-law relationship with my children's father.

"What's wrong with being in a common-law relationship?" I needed to know.

"It causes people to commit sexual immorality."

"What is so wrong with being sexually intimate with someone that you love?"

"Nothing… if you are married to that person," he answered.

"But why is it necessary to be married? Even the law states that when two people live together long enough, they are considered to be the equivalent of married, by becoming common-law? So why do we still have to go through the official ceremony?"

"Because, when you're married to that person, God blesses the union. If He hasn't blessed the union, then it is not blessed, and therefore it is…"

"…cursed?" I answered.

"That's right."

All that Mark shared was difficult to ignore. It was too accurate and detailed to be coincidental. It was becoming clear to me why all these things had gone so terribly wrong in my life for so many years.

"Are you absolutely positive living a homosexual lifestyle will result in me not inheriting this Kingdom of God and blessed life?" I questioned one final time.

Mark opened the Bible resting on his lap, and quoted: "... *Do not be deceived: neither the...immoral... nor those who participate in homosexuality... will inherit or have any share in the kingdom of God.*" [7]

It became clear I should not have ignored that statement when I heard it all those years ago. Or at the very least, I should have taken the time to look into what it truly meant instead of just making the decision to ignore it.

Changes in legislation—harmful, helpful or an illusion?

I pressed the question to Mark, asking why legislation had been changed in regard to same-sex relationships and common-law marriage if doing so went against divine law.

Mark simply pointed out that oftentimes, political representatives are not aware of divine laws and principles. I was shocked to think this. I did not know much about the constitution, but I did know that it was sourced from the Bible, so I assumed that representatives charged with upholding the constitution would be required to know at least some biblical truth, thereby remaining bound to the basis it was founded upon and to stay legitimately in the best interest of society.

I learned that with each change in the constitution—whether to a rule, regulation, law or bylaw, be it state, provincial, or municipal government—every single change begins with one person's opinion. More astonishing, that one person can have an opinion that opposes and rejects the original legislative decisions of our political forefathers.

"So if someone doesn't want to abide by any currently existing legislative rule or regulation, they can choose to fight against it, and keep on fighting; drawing up petitions, soliciting signatures, and remaining tenacious until the legislation is changed?" I questioned for verification.

"Yes," Mark confirmed. "Historically, the result has been, rather than governmental officials learning about divine laws and principles, along with the potential curses for not following them and declaring such laws unchangeable on those grounds, there have been officials who have chosen instead to simply change the current law or legislation to appease people simply to win votes, get elected, or get re-elected."

"What ability, trait or qualification did an opposing person have that made him or her more powerful or authoritative than our political forefathers who based their laws on God's truth, who wrote the constitution to begin with?" I asked.

"The answer is simple" he answered, "the opposing person's refusal to desist. Such a person keeps fighting until what he or she wants is received, regardless of what is right, wrong, or in the best interest of society."

I was astonished to learn this.

Although I had been part of changing legislation of same-sex rights all those years ago, I honestly believed at the time that the law would not be changed if it went against what was truly right and what could cause anyone harm.

Knowing that such laws have been approved and passed by government in certain areas has made it evidently clear that I, and society, did nothing more than buy into the illusion that these laws were changeable to begin with.

Chapter Eight

A New Beginning

It takes a great deal of strength and courage.

I sat quietly for a moment pondering and absorbing all that Mark had shared with me.

"Mark?" I finally said, "I've been living here for a year, yet I'm just learning about all this information now. Why have you not told me all of this before?"

"You never asked." He softly replied.

"Where do I even begin to make a change?" I queried.

"Start by using your free will to stop living your life your way, and to start living it God's way."

"How can I be sure if I stop being gay, my life will turn around?"

"Without faith you cannot be sure," he replied. "That's the hard part. All you can do is believe and trust that if you stop, He *will* turn your life around and give you back everything you've lost and fix all that is broken. Many people believe it is only the weak, timid and distraught who turn to God for help, guidance and direction. The reality is, it takes a great deal of strength and courage to turn your life over to Him."

I knew in my heart he was speaking the truth.

"What do I do about these strong homosexual desires and feelings I've had for the past 13 years?" I needed to know.

"Ask God to take away those desires, and He will." He answered.

"It's that simple?" I questioned, finding it hard to believe it would be that easy.

"Yes, it's that simple." He said with a smile.

"Will all those feelings go away immediately?" I needed to know.

"The strong desire will." He answered. Letting me know our desire is what is implanted deeply within us. Feelings on the other hand are more on the surface and influenced by our senses—what we see, hear and feel. God would do His part and take away the strong desire. It would then be up to me to resist the temptations and feelings coming at me through my senses.

He told me if I did my part, soon all my homosexual desires and feelings would be completely gone.

Getting my life back.

A few days later, on March 25, 2005 we all got together to celebrate Mark's birthday. We enjoyed all the customary birthday rituals for a 40-something year old, but what happened later that day made it really memorable for all of us.

As we all sat together in the family room, the topic of committing to being in relationship with God was brought up. Mark's two eldest children, both still young teenagers, showed an interest in making this commitment in their lives. I was more than interested as well. I did not know all that it would entail, but I had witnessed the great calm, peace and tranquility this family fostered on a daily basis and I was altogether interested in bringing some of whatever it was that they had into my own life.

Mark gathered us all together, close to him. He began to pray over us. I put myself at ease. I was not sure exactly what was about to happen, but I was ready to try anything in order to get my life back. He asked us to repeat after him, which we did. He said, *"God I have been a sinner..."* (which I did not like to say), *"... my life is broken and a mess"* (which was so true). *"I don't want to be this way anymore"* (which I was happy to say). *"I ask You to take my broken, messed up life and fix it."* (Oh, how I desperately longed to have the mess of my life and brokenness fixed.) *"Take me just the way I am."* (I felt so vulnerable, just like a child reaching up for help and support.) *"Come into my life,"* (Yes, please. I felt a calmness and peace overtake me that I had never felt before.) *"Make me who You want me to be."* (I completely surrendered my will over to whatever His will would be for my life. If He was truly willing to take the lead, I was ready to let Him.) *"I make You my Lord and Saviour."* (I was more than willing to allow Him to be in charge for a change.) *"In Jesus' Name, Amen."* (Amen!)

For the first time in my life, I felt hopeful that now my life might actually turn out right.

I felt an immediate calm within me. A sense of carefree joy washed over me. It was like, at that moment, I did not have a care in the world. I believe it was the first time that I actually sensed true peace and calm. Tears streamed down my face and when I looked up to both Mark and Sarah, I saw their happiness for me. I had done this for me. They never told me to do it; they were just there for me to help me discover this amazing truth.

Although I still barely knew anything about God, I felt somewhat connected with Him. If He was willing to come into my life and fix up the mess I had made of it, then that was where I wanted Him to be.

"So what do I do now?" I asked.

"Trust Him," Mark replied, "and keep praying."

"I'm not sure I know how."

"Prayer is simply communication between you and God" he told me. "Just talk to Him like you would a friend. Let Him know what you desire, then listen and He will talk to you. Then do whatever He tells you to do."

"Isn't it a little weird to hear voices? And how can I be sure God is speaking and that it isn't just my own thoughts?"

"God's voice will always lead us to the solution, and to what is right," he assured me. Then he pointed out the whole point of prayer is to receive answers.

I had never thought about that before. I had learned I was supposed to pray, but was never taught to expect God to respond.

I heard a still small voice.

After hugs and thanks, I retired to my room. Though I did not know what to expect, I was uplifted from the entire experience. I nestled into my bed; just before I fell asleep, I said a prayer. It was very simple: "God, thank you for coming into my life. I need your help. I think I'm ready to move out now, but I need that money. Can you please help me?" Then I closed my eyes and went to sleep.

At 3:00 a.m., I awoke from a sound sleep. I was not groggy, but totally alert. I heard a still small voice say, "*Look on the back of the cheque.*" That was all the voice said. I got up, walked over to that $5,000 photocopy of the cheque that had been cashed by the woman I had lent the money to, two years prior. It had been there on top of my desk for weeks now. I flipped it over. I saw on the back of the photocopied cheque, all the vital information that I had been searching for to get the funds released to me. It had the bank stamp containing the bank address and location, the branch number and the account number.

The information had been in my possession all along, but I had not noticed it on the back of the photocopy, nor had Sarah (always the inquisitive one, who loved investigating), nor had the court clerk from the courthouse. I was shocked, yet thankful. I knew there was nothing more I could do at that moment, so I placed the photocopied cheque back on the desk and fell back into a sound, restful sleep.

When I awoke, I could not wait to tell Sarah and Mark about what had happened. After I shared what happened, Mark said something about what had transpired that made a profound impression on me.

"That's what being in a relationship with God is all about!" he said. "Think about it. The Creator of the universe spoke directly to you last night. That's how much He loves you."

That was when I came to the full realization that the previous night, I had made the best decision of my entire life. I knew for the first time that God really was real, and that He really does talk to us. I had prayed many times in my life before this, but had never received a response as evident as this was, nor had I ever heard His voice as clearly as I had that night.

Sarah and Mark let me know we can ask for God's help in every area of our life, and He will help us. He will show us things we could not see before, and repair or restore whatever is broken, missing, or lost so that our life can be happy and complete. He will cause things to happen that we cannot possibly make happen on our own. They also told me I could not offend Him with my prayers and that I could pray for anything. If it was His will, they said, I would have it. If it was not His will, I would not.

I had nothing to lose, so I began to pray for good things to start happening in every area of my life. I wanted to have my children back and living with me; I hoped that it was still possible, and not too late. I wanted a nice home for them, and for that home to serve as a perfect place for me to work and provide childcare. I wanted money to pay down my debt; in fact, I prayed that I would be completely debt-free. I wanted to regain my health and needed healing for my shoulder. Finally, I wanted to be able to pay back Sarah and Mark for all the money that they had loaned to me. I also felt I owed them a fair amount for all their graciousness and kindness in housing me and feeding me for all those months. I really hoped to provide this in one large sum, rather than in small installments. In order to be able to do all this, I would need that money very soon, so I prayed for God to help me get that money quickly. I hoped that all this would be in His will for my life, because this was truly what I desired in my heart. Lastly, knowing it was God's will—I prayed for Him to take away the homosexual desire from within me.

He's working behind the scenes.

The following business day I took the photocopy of the cheque and walked back into the courthouse. I was directed to the woman's bank to claim my money. I carried with me the court order, as evidence of my authority to claim the funds. I was able to meet with the manager of her bank.

I ran into a glitch when I was faced with the fact that due to court legalities, I was unable to walk away with the funds that day. I had to wait until the bank could contact the courthouse to confirm the information I provided. Then they would forward the money to another department to process, and they would then mail it to my home. The process would take approximately six weeks.

Sarah reassured me that sometimes things do not go exactly as we plan, but that I would receive that money when the time was right.

Now hopeful that this process would provide me with funds soon, I began to search for a place to live. A few days later, Sarah passed a house with a rental sign posted out front. She let me know about it. The house was in a great neighborhood and seemed like the perfect place to provide childcare. I was so excited; I asked if she would drive me there so I could see it as soon as possible. A few minutes later, we pulled up in front of it.

From the outside, it looked perfect. In my excitement, I boldly strode up to the front door and rang the doorbell. A woman answered the door. From the doorway, I could see sunlight streaming in through the rear patio doors. It felt welcoming and inviting. I asked if I could make an appointment to see the place. Graciously, she allowed me right in to view it immediately.

As soon as I stepped inside, I knew this was the place for me—for us. It was everything I had hoped for. The foyer was exactly as I had imagined, with a place to add a gate to ensure the children's safety. It had a washroom on the main floor, near the living room, which I would convert into the children's playroom. Next to that was the kitchen, adorned in a tasteful Mexican mosaic design. Just off that was the dining room, bathed in sunlight from the large patio doors overlooking the completely secured and enclosed backyard. Upstairs, there were three bedrooms, including a master bedroom with an ensuite. It had everything I imagined, including two rooms for my children, should they ever return to live with me.

It was perfect! The rent was within my budget, and the owners were gracious, thoughtful and considerate. I could not have asked for more. I desperately wanted this place.

When we walked out, Sarah turned to me and asked what I thought about the place. All she had to do at that moment was see the expression on my face and she knew that I absolutely loved it.

The only problem was, the house would be available in less than two weeks. If I did not have the money by then, I could potentially lose the place. It had been only a few days since I had returned from the courthouse, so I knew the $5,000 owed me would not arrive for another 5-6 weeks.

Accustomed to dealing with these sorts of things on my own, I immediately went into panic mode and my old way of thinking. I began trying to figure this out on my own.

Sarah calmed me down and reminded me that trying to figure it all out would essentially just be me doing things "my way." She then forewarned me that it would also potentially land me in the same sort of mess I had been in before. She reminded me that the right thing to do was to let God take the lead and trust that He would make it all work out.

This was defiantly challenging—I never thought that doing nothing but trusting could be so challenging.

I knew the property owners were performing their due diligence by conducting a credit check and verifying the references I had provided to them. I was tempted to be nervous about that, knowing it would not look very good, due to all the financial difficulties I had endured over the last dozen years. Sarah reassured me that I had nothing to worry about.

A few days later, I received a phone call from the woman's husband. They had checked my credit. I held my breath for a moment. By now, I wanted this place more than any other I had seen. I hoped they would call with good news. "Your credit check cleared and we would like to offer you the house," he said, letting me know I could move in at the beginning of the month. All they required was first and last months' rent.

I stood silent for a moment. Though elated that my credit check had cleared, worry tried to set back in. The beginning of the month was a little over one week away, and my $5,000 check was still an estimated five weeks away. I thanked them for their call and agreed to meet them at month end to sign the rental agreement.

I turned to Sarah. "How am I ever going to get this money in time?"

"Don't worry," she reminded me. "God is your partner now. Just trust that He's working behind the scenes for you.

And whenever you're tempted to worry, just talk to Him, He'll tell you what to do."

The number on the letter.

This proved to be the right advice, because as the days passed, and the continued hope of having this place still held my heart, I enjoyed a state of relaxed peace. I did not stress or worry—not that I wasn't tempted to—but whenever I felt the urge to stress, I would simply ask God: "What should I do?"

The response I would hear was, "Do nothing, just wait."

I would take a deep breath and force myself not to do anything but wait.

Sarah and Mark helped a lot during this time, by not doing anything except simply reminding me to trust. If God wanted me to do something, He would surely let me know, they reminded me. I continued to follow their lead and allowed myself not to struggle or fret over thoughts of what I should do or could do. I simply practiced doing absolutely nothing except trusting. Whenever I would get anxious, I would pray quietly, "What should I do?"

Inevitably the response would be, "Nothing...just wait."

As the days passed, I began to struggle more and more to fend off anxiety, but I continued to do exactly what Sarah and Mark told me to do. I prayed, "What should I do?"

Each time, I would inevitably hear back: "Wait."

I had been checking the mail every single day in the hope that the cheque would arrive. It reached the 27th day of the month, and still no cheque had arrived. As I had been doing all along, I stood at the mailbox with no cheque in hand and prayed once again, "What should I do?"

This time when the answer came back, it was different. I heard a voice say to me, "Call about the cheque."

"Call who?" I quickly asked.

"Call the number on the letter."

Until that moment, I had forgotten all about the letter I had received from the courthouse. I had simply filed it along with the banking information of the bank holding the funds. I immediately went back into the house and found the letter. At the bottom was contact information about who to reach to find out the status of my case. It was 8 a.m., and their office promised to open at that time.

He had been waiting for me.

I called and was immediately connected to a live voice (amazing). As had always been my experience when calling government offices, I had expected to be greeted by an auto attendant, and then placed on hold for an extraordinarily long time. Yet here I was, speaking to a woman, person to person, who answered before the third ring! I mentioned my amazement to her. She admitted that it was a rarity. She had just arrived and my call snuck in just before she initiated the call answer system. I was thankful for this.

I told her my name and let her know my situation concerning the court paper, the meeting with the bank, and the townhouse I needed a deposit for—in three days. I asked if there was anything she could do to help me. She asked me to repeat my name. When I did, she responded by saying that my information was right there, at the top of her pile. Once again, we were both slightly amazed.

I asked her if she could expedite the processing of this paperwork, and send the cheque in time for me to receive it in three days. She let me know that typically, that was not the case, and informed me of the steps it would involve. She would need to process it, and then it would be sent to another department to be verified. It would be ready to leave her offices within another two to four weeks. Two weeks after that, I would receive it, depending on the mail service. Although I was glad she was being honest, I was slightly discouraged to learn the process, and how long it would take.

Somehow, hope rose up within me and I asked her once again if she could possibly make an exception and expedite this matter for me as soon as possible so that, hopefully, I would receive it within three days. She let me know that since this was such an unusual case—her actually having picked up the phone call and the paperwork being found there on the top of the pile—that she would do her best to get this cheque into the mail that very same day! I thanked her, then hung up the phone.

I immediately turned to Sarah in amazement at what had just transpired. She just looked at me and smiled saying, "See what God can do when you let Him?"

I realized that oftentimes in my past, I had been waiting for God to do something in my life, but now I realized that He had been waiting for me.

PAID IN FULL

For the next three days, I remained hopeful, against all odds. Not only did I hope that the government worker I had spoken with would follow through with what she promised, but also that the next department would find the urgency in this matter and expedite it just as quickly. Finally, I hoped that the mail service—though it could have no way of knowing the urgency—would also process my letter and deliver it to me within three days. Whenever I had the urge to worry or fret, I would remind myself how much His hand was already in this situation, and that reality calmed me.

I knew there was absolutely nothing more I could do at this time but wait patiently; I had done my part, now I needed to trust God to do His part.

Exactly three days later, the cheque arrived in the mail!

This was no small miracle for me, considering all that had happened in order to get this to me on time.

With the cheque in hand, I met with my future landlords the same afternoon and presented them with the first and last month's rent. We signed the lease agreement and the place was now officially mine.

Returning back to Sarah and Mark's home, I walked in the door and presented them with a cheque for over $2,000 to repay them the money that I owed to them. To impress the point on me, after I handed the cheque to them, Mark wrote in big red letters across the account of all the monies owed: *PAID IN FULL.* I started to feel like my life was finally heading in the proper direction.

The $5,000 I had loaned to a fellow business associate (with the best intentions), had returned to me at the most opportune time.

I learned that in my own ability, I am very limited and often faced with things that seem impossible, but with God on my side, all things are possible. I could now better understand the relationship people claimed they had with Him; I was both shocked and pleasantly surprised to discover it really works.

Perfectly, painlessly, and effortlessly.

I was excited and truly happy to be in this new phase of life. I was very much at peace in my new home. The only thing missing was my children. It had been six years since they last lived with me and they were now 15 and 17. Every time I went upstairs to my own room, I had to pass the empty bedrooms off the middle of the hallway. I knew the likelihood of my children even desiring to return to me was getting slimmer with each passing day, but I remained hopeful my prayer had been heard all those years ago when I had to let them go.

One day, an announcer on local radio said something that got me running for pen and paper. Luckily, he chose to repeat it all again, otherwise I would have missed it for sure. He was quoting Blaise Pascal, an influential French mathematician and philosopher who lived in the 1600s. Although I could not quite catch the exact quote, this is what I understood he said about the relevance of God:

If you live your life as if God DOES exist

and He DOES, then you get everything.

And, if you live your life as if God DOES exist

and He does NOT, then you have lost nothing.

However, if you live your life as if God does NOT exist

and He does NOT, then it didn't matter anyway.

But, if you live your life as if God does NOT exist

and He DOES, then you Lose Everything!

With everything I had gained and lost (then gained) in my life, I believed what he said to be true. The last stanza especially made the most sense to me.

I knew I did not know everything that I needed to know, but I knew one thing for sure: what Mark had been talking about, and what Jenny had shown by example, was working for me. I was seeing results, just as they had promised. I had trusted and believed, even when it did not make sense. I had faith in what I could not yet see, and worked hard at doing what was right, even when that meant doing nothing at all.

All my life I believed if I wanted something done right, I would have to do it myself. I knew now that often we face things that are completely out of our control. Through the entire $5,000 ordeal, I experienced a brand new way of thinking and dealing with a challenging situation. That experience gave me hope that I had not known before, hope in something that would have been impossible for me in my own power. Hope that with God's help, everything else in my life would also come together perfectly, painlessly, and effortlessly.

Chapter Nine

Beneficial Effects

I could see something I had not seen before.

After all that I had learned and all that had transpired in my life, I found myself in one final, old familiar situation. Only this time, I could finally see things differently.

It was Christmas Eve 2007 and I was attending a midnight church service with my twenty year old son, and my eighteen year old daughter. I had chosen the church because of the choir (seriously)! Other than that, I did not want to be there.

My son was already living on his own and had recently joined the Canadian Reserves. My daughter had completed high school and let me know just a few months earlier that she would be moving away the following summer. Realistically, I knew the chances of them returning every year at Christmastime, despite their best intentions, would not always be possible.

In light of not knowing what the future held for us, I decided to make our "final" Christmas Eve together a memorable one. Traditionally, we had gone to a huge Christmas Eve service in downtown Toronto, hosted by the gay preacher of the gay church I used to attend (who had now received his Doctor of Ministry degree). Though it was not my first choice to take them there, I knew they would enjoy the music and maybe even the sermon. I had been out of the gay lifestyle for well over two years by now, but I believed there was a reason I was compelled to go to that final Christmas Eve service with them.

The title of the sermon was "Can One Child Make a Difference?" I listened intently as he spoke about exactly that. But something was different that night from all the other Christmas Eve sermons I had heard from him. In fact, something was different than all the other sermons I had ever heard him preach. My blinders had been removed and for the first time in 15 years, I saw something I had never seen before.

As he spoke about one child making a difference, I felt very strongly that he was not talking about the birth of Jesus Christ, but rather that he was talking about himself. My suspicion grew as he told of his latest achievement, and then with pride, pointed to a pin on his lapel symbolizing some measure of achievement he had recently received with respect to making some advancement within the homosexual community. I could see for the first time that this preacher was not here for the sake and protection of the congregation—he could not possibly be; otherwise, he would teach them the truth.

Proven: What Mark had been telling me.

As the congregation clapped for the preacher's sermon, my daughter leaned over to me and asked, "Why don't you go to this church anymore?"

Though I had never been asked this question before, my answer came quickly to me.

I turned to her and said, "I originally came to this church to learn the truth and to make sure God approved of me being a homosexual. I trusted this preacher to tell me the absolute truth, but instead he deceived me; he taught me that God approves of homosexuals—which He does. But he failed to mention that homosexual behavior is not acceptable—which was a huge misrepresentation of the truth. Because I chose to trust him without doubt or question, it resulted in my life being cursed."

I pointed into the congregation and said, "I'm sure many of these people have also trusted him and been deceived like I was, and their lives are now being cursed."

Even though these words came from my own lips, they burned in my ears. I knew then and there the reason I had gone there that night. It was not just me who had been deceived and suffered my life being cursed. The entire congregation had been subjected to the same misrepresentation of the truth as I had. No doubt, they had entered this church at some point in their life with the same intention and purpose I had—to ensure they were not living their lives against the will of God. Now they, along with everyone else who received this misrepresentation of truth including government officials, educators, and the media, had also been duped like I was.

I realized how truly fortunate I had been to have had the opportunity to live with a Christian family and witness for myself the good life—the way our lives are meant to be. Everything I had learned, experienced, and tested out for myself proved what Mark had been telling me was the absolute truth. I realized then that many others would not get the same opportunity I had, but they deserved to know the truth as well.

I thought back to that other church moment that changed my life, when my ex common-law husband asked me: "Who put you in charge?" Now I finally had an answer to that question as well: "God did." He put each of us in charge of our own life, by giving us the free will to learn the truth, so we can make right choices and reap all the benefits and rewards of living the good life we were intended to live all along.

Reaping the rewards of living a blessed life.

I have experienced life and over its course, unknowingly, have broken many divine laws and principles along the way. As a result, my life was cursed and torn apart. Everything I held dear was taken away from me.

Now that I am aware of what it means to live a prosperous spiritual lifestyle, I choose to live my life that way and my life is truly blessed. Not only am I prosperous in all areas of life now but I have regained everything I lost, including everything that was broken and missing. My life is now a peaceful, yet exciting journey, and it continuously gets better each and every day.

Here are some of the blessings I have received.

Relationship with family

At the age of 16, my daughter was returned back home to me by the desire that was planted in her heart. Since then our mother/daughter relationship has grown and strengthened exponentially into an amazing, respectful friendship, far beyond anything I could have ever dreamed of, hoped for, or imagined.

I lost my son when he was 11. By the age of 18, he had completed high school. After that, he moved out on his own for four years. It appeared my opportunity to ever have him return home was long gone.

At age 22, by his own free will choice, my son also returned home. My prayer was answered. I have since learned that one of the divine principles states when we lose something we should not have lost; we will receive double back in return. This came to pass when I lost my son at 11 — he was returned to me at 22.

I am so blessed to have had both of my children return home to live with me. Even though each of them has moved out since then, their return fulfilled the prayer I had kept in my heart. That precious time we spent together rekindled and fixed our broken relationship and now I have the relationship and family life with my children I had always hoped for—one of mutual honor, respect and unconditional love towards one another.

Money and Debt-Freedom

I have learned we are not supposed to be poor, broke or indebted. Understanding and following the divine law of money has rendered me consumer debt-free. When I opened up a business and operated my finances my way, I landed in $75,000 worth of debt. When I did it God's way, I received job stability (even through the recession) and I got out of $75,000 worth of debt.

Divine laws and principles will work for anybody. I have learned many people follow the divine law of money—whether knowingly or unknowingly—and have become very wealthy.

Health and Healing

Since I follow the divine laws and principles of health and healing, my health has been regained, and my body has been healed. The injury I sustained in my left shoulder diagnosed as bursitis has been completely healed; medical reports show no evidence of any injury or abnormality. My memory has been restored and my thinking is clear. My health is now strong and I am no longer sickly and allergic to a huge list of things that I suffered from for so many years.

My personal lifestyle choice

I have learned that when we choose to live our life God's way, He does many things behind the scenes to bless our lives. When I first made the decision to no longer live a homosexual lifestyle, I was concerned it would be difficult to convert. The truth is, when I asked God to take away the homosexual desire, it was not difficult. Now those desires and feelings are completely gone. I can still see beauty and attractiveness in a woman, but I am no longer drawn in by a wrong desire.

When asked whether or not I am straight, the answer is yes, I am now straight; both by the world's standard and by God's standard. It is His will that we live a straight life. Since I am no longer bound by wrong desires, I am free to live my life the way I was born to live it—blessed, not cursed.

The love of my children and the love of God fill my life with joy, happiness, peace, serenity and comfort. If it is His will for me to be in a relationship with someone in the future, then I would look forward to sharing and enjoying our lives together. But I have learned to pray, then wait for Him to direct my steps. In the meantime I am not out searching, since that would be doing things my way. Instead I am simply patiently waiting and trusting that God is working behind the scenes in this area; believing whatever His will is for my life, it will come to pass when the time is right. While I am waiting, I am living and thoroughly enjoying this blessed life.

In Conclusion

I used to think people who chose to live their lives God's way were missing out on life. Now I know that is true—they are missing out on being ruled over by fear, frustration, stress, confusion, anger, anxiety, loss, hurt, pain and many other undesirable things. What these people are not missing out on is fun, laughter, peace, joy, happiness, enjoyment of life, and an abundance of all good things.

Now this is not to suggest living the right way exempts people from having to deal with unexpected challenges, experience pain, or have disappointments; but when this happens, they can be at peace, have restful sleep, and even have joy while they are going through whatever they are facing—knowing that God is working behind the scenes, fixing whatever is broken and causing things to happen that they could not possibly do on their own.

I share all this with you because God is no respecter of persons. We were all created equal and are all similarly important to Him. What He did for me, He will do for you... if you let Him.

I have learned that nothing is hopeless, impossible, and it is never too late.

We have all been given free will to choose the life we live. Now it is up to each of us to choose wisely!

Endnotes

Bibliography

Random House Webster's college dictionary – 2nd. Ed.
New York: Random House. 1997

Nanny McPhee, Dir. Kirk Jones, Starring Emma Thompson,
Universal Pictures, 2005